Physical Characte...istics of the
Boxer
(from the American Kennel ...

M000013750

Topline: Smooth, firm and slightly sloping.

Tail: Set high, docked and carried upward.

Hindquarters: The hindquarters are strongly muscled with angulation in balance with that of the forequarters. The thighs are broad and curved. Leg well angulated at the stifle with a clearly defined, well "let down" hock joint.

Color: The colors are fawn and brindle. White markings should be of such distribution as to enhance the dog's appearance, but may not exceed one-third of the entire coat.

Coat: Short, shiny, lying smooth and tight to the body.

Height: Adult males 22.5 to 25 inches; females 21 to 23.5 inches.

Feet: Compact, turning neither in nor out, with well arched toes.

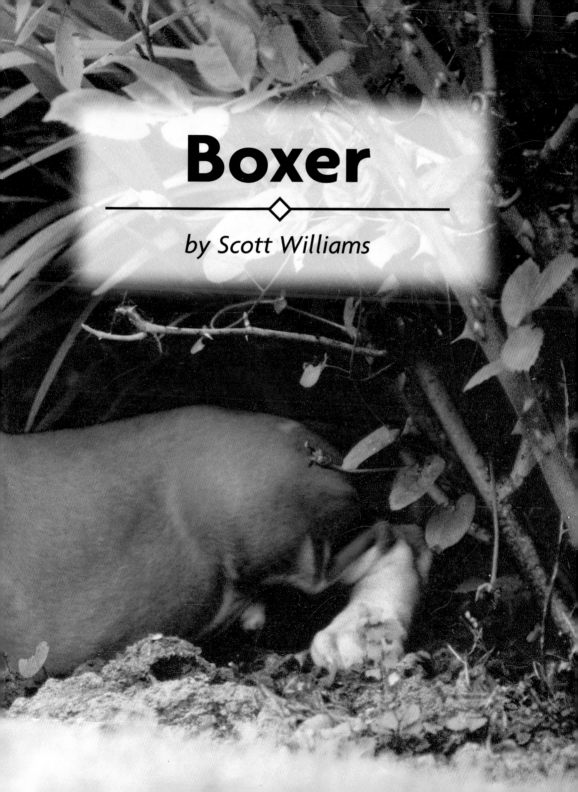

Boxer

◇

by Scott Williams

Boxer

Contents

KENNEL CLUB BOOKS® BOXER
ISBN: 1-59378-206-3

Copyright © 2003, 2007 • Kennel Club Books® • A Division of BowTie, Inc.
40 Main Street, Freehold, NJ 07728 USA
Cover Design Patented: US 6,435,559 B2 • Printed in South Korea

Photos by Norvia Behling, Carolina Biological Supply, Doskocil, Theresa Fico, Isabelle Français, James Hayden-Yoav, James R. Hayden, RBP, Carol Ann Johnson, The *Journal of the American Veterinary Medicine Association*, Dwight R. Kuhn, Dr. Dennis Kunkel, Jeff Michals, Mikki Pet Products, Alice Pantfoeder, Antonio Philippe, Phototake, Jean Claude Revy, Alice Roche, Paul Scott, Dr. Andrew Spielman, M.A. Stevenson, DVM, Nikki Sussman, Alice van Kempen and C. James Webb.

Illustrations by Patricia Peters.

Today's elegant Boxer is light years from the breed's ancestors who were bred to hunt boars, pigs and deer. The Boxer breed, beloved around the world, excels as a show dog, obedience performance dog and, of course, as a home companion and guard dog.

History of the Boxer

Most dog historians acknowledge that the Boxer derives from Bullenbeisser ancestry. These Bullenbeissers, or bull-biters, were hunting dogs, mostly used on pig, boar and deer. Such wild-game expeditions often cost the lives of many dogs, as the hunt was gruesome and grueling for humans and dogs alike—not to mention the boars! Some sources say that these massive medieval dogs had erect ears and huge teeth, which would be used to hold the animal by the nose. It's probable that hunters were cropping ears the way we do today, since such a custom would be apropos for these hunting dogs.

Not all generations of dogs have lived in civilized times like our own! It's always the contention of the living that their times are the most civilized and

Boxers of fine quality are available not only in Germany but also throughout Europe, America and elsewhere. This is Int. Ch. Formula Miller of Norwegian and Canadian origin.

The name "Boxer" translates from the German as "mutt": not a very high compliment to the refined breed of dog we recognize today.

dog pit, battling fellow canines. The "sport" of dog fighting followed swiftly on the heels of animal baiting. Dog fights became even more in vogue! In some countries today, including such civilized nations as the US, such heinous sporting still goes on, albeit illegally. By the mid-nineteenth century, bull baiting as well as dog fighting were banned in Germany, the Boxer's homeland.

On a more civilized and utilitarian route, the Boxer's ancestors were commonly employed as butcher dogs, for their ability to hold a bull and drive the animal into its pen, should it become unruly. The famous reputation of the dog named "Boxl," used by a butcher in Berlin, is credited for

acceptable of all times in history. The ancestors of our beloved Boxers did not have it so easy. They came about at a time when humans were obsessed with "blood sports." The baiting of bulls and bears was a mainstream attraction, and dogs that were strong, agile and fearless were needed to win and to keep the paying audience aroused. Fortunately for our friend the Boxer, his ancestors were not ideally suited for this bloody pastime: they were neither agile enough nor small enough to dodge the horns and hooves of the poor captive bull, which passionately was trying to protect itself from the jaws of the dogs. The smaller dogs were quicker and more inclined to fight "head on." These miniature gladiators (weighing approximately 35 to 55 pounds) would excel in the

PLANNED PAIRINGS

It was only in the 19th century that humans really took notice of the dogs around them, and how they looked, what color they were and how big they were. Dogs all along have been helpmates—some dogs hunted, some killed vermin and some dogs protected property. No one bred the big black dog to the big black bitch because they were both black and big, necessarily. More than likely, humans paired dogs for their abilities. To produce a strong, protective dog, they would mate two dogs with those desirable qualities. Thus were progenerated various dogs with superior abilities.

giving the breed its name. The derivation of the word "Boxer" for a pure-bred dog is ironical, since the term "boxl" or "boxel" essentially translates to "mutt!" In 1894, a famous German breeder of Bulldogs, Friedrich Roberth, was the first to coin the name "Boxer" in print. His article, which ran in a local paper, complimented the Boxer for its intelligence and appearance, ranking the dog higher than any of the other breeds Roberth had owned, which were considerable. He acknowledged, however, that his Boxer bitch had a cleft palate and loose shoulder, but otherwise was very impressive to all who met her. He also states that there were no breeders of the German Boxer who were pursuing a serious program, adding that it was rare to get a litter with more than one or two good pups. Roberth's article concluded with a plea for any established, knowledgeable dog person to initiate a club for the Boxer in Germany. As is the case in the dog world today, a new breed is best established by persons already "in the fancy." Roberth knew that this was the only viable way for a new breed to take hold in Germany.

Fortunately, the Germans have never been slow to form a committee! Thus, within one year of Roberth's plea, the Munich Boxer Club was formed in 1895. At the first dog show that allowed Boxers (with an entry of four!),

The first dog show in which Boxers participated may well have been in Munich, Germany in 1895. Boxers have undergone serious changes since that time and today's Boxers are much more uniform in terms of size, structure and personality.

Flocki, owned by G. Muhlbauer of Munich, was the first Boxer to win a class. Roberth and a handful of fanciers began the German Boxer Club later that year, and Roberth was called upon to draft a standard for the breed. A standard is a written description of how an ideal specimen of the breed should appear; such a document, once endorsed by the club, becomes the measuring stick for

breeders and judges. The first sentence of this early standard still perfectly describes our Boxer: "The outward appearance should be of a compact, solid, sturdy, powerful and active dog that stands proudly and moves on straight healthy legs."

This standard was based on the Boxer that was regarded as the best dog around at that time. His name was Flock St. Salvador, and he won the first show for Boxers in 1896. The famous German Boxer magazine, *Der Boxer Blatter,* was established in 1904 and is still published today.

The dog that would become the most important stud dog in the breed is Ch. Rolf v. Vogelsberg, owned by Philip Stockmann, regarded as "the father of the Boxer." His wife, equally famous, was Friederun Miriam Stockmann, who continued to make their von Dom kennel famous after Philip's death. In World War I, the Boxer was fast chosen as a military dog and messenger dog. The Stockmanns provided many Boxers for the military, and the drafted Philip worked as a trainer for the services, leaving Frau Stockmann alone to handle the kennels. The war was claiming most usable Boxers for sentry and guard duty against snipers. Among the first dogs selected were the able and proven Boxer champions, given the breed's robustness and athletic

The German Boxer was used for bull-baiting, the same as the British Bulldog, in the 1890s.

The German Boxer of 1905 showed more prominent Boston Terrier features than modern Boxers display.

ability. According to German Kennel Club regulations, the title of champion also required the dog to be of fit, working ability, so champions were the obvious first choice as they were already versed in Schutzhund or similar-type obedience training. Many of the dogs that served in the military died in service, including hundreds of family pets. Rolf von Vogelsberg proved his worth as a war dog, and lived to tell about it (he also sired a couple of litters during the course of the war!). As a show dog, he was undefeated and secured five championships (the last of which was won after the war).

Shortly after the war, the Stockmanns' reputation for excellent Boxers was far-reaching, and many wealthy Americans sought German-bred Boxers to improve their breeding programs. Frau Stockmann, who had endured many hardships with the war and had little money to keep her kennel running, was forced to sell some of her best dogs, not the least of which was Ch. Sigurd von Dom, one of her most promising

The early German Boxers in the 1900s were characterized by this famous photo of Dr. Grete Maria Ehrenstein, a famous Viennese beauty, and her dog. Note that the dogs' ears were cropped even then!

stud dogs, followed by the great Ch. Lustig von Dom, considered to be the most influential Boxer of all time. It was the Tulgey Wood Kennels in America that purchased Lustig, and this line would eventually yield the greatest show dog of all time, Ch. Bang Away of Sirrah Crest, a dog that is still regarded today as the ultimate Boxer.

World War II reduced Frau Stockmann to desperate measures, even though her Boxers were among the dogs deemed worthy to be fed. The German government designated which breeds, based on their utility, were cost-effective to sustain. The Boxer was the number-two breed selected, on the

MILITARY DOGS

Boxers have been used as military dogs since World War I. Their roles have been numerous. The dogs served as sentries, guards, mine detectors, rescuers of wounded soldiers and carriers of food and medicine.

The German Boxer of 1903 was a robust, athletic dog.

The expression of a good Boxer should be proud and alert.

troops stationed in Germany greatly admired the Boxer, and many drab-green passers-by told the Frau that the Boxer was the number-one breed in America. Frau Stockmann relished hearing about the Boxer's popularity in America, knowing that her beloved breed would continue worldwide years after she was gone.

A few years later, Frau Stockmann was invited to the United States, where she judged the breed and was gifted with dogs by some of America's top breeders. While in the States, she also had the opportunity to judge the three-month-old Bang Away of Sirrah Crest. She awarded him Best Puppy in Match, over 110 puppies, and referred to him as "Little Lustig." Her eye for a dog was never more precise, as Bang Away would go on to earn a record-breaking 121 Best in Show awards, including the famous Westminster Kennel Club.

heels of the German Shepherd Dog. Frau Stockmann trained dogs for messenger service, which required that the dogs perform under the "distraction" of gunfire. The Boxer proved particularly adept, not surprisingly. American

THE BOXER IN THE UNITED KINGDOM

Philip Stockmann, the famous German breeder of Boxers, fretted over the breed's name in his book *My Life with Boxers*. He bemoaned that this valiant German dog has an English name! The Boxer, we must admit, does have ties to the United Kingdom, and there's more than a little Bull-dog in the Boxer's blood.

The first imported Boxer arrived in Britain in 1933, when it was registered with The Kennel Club. In 1939, the first champion was recorded: Eng. Ch. Horsa of Leith Hill, bred by Mrs. D. Sprig, the first secretary of the British Boxer Club, which was founded three years earlier in 1936. Despite Horsa's accomplishment, he would have no lasting influence on the Boxer breed in England, as the breed remained in relative obscurity until after World War II.

From 1936 to 1953, Allon Dawson of the Stainburndorf prefix imported many Boxers into Britain from Germany, Holland and the US, the most important of which was Ch. Zunftig von Dom, son of Lustig, bred by the Stock-

A lovely modern British Boxer shows off his flashy markings.

WHAT IS SCHUTZHUND?

In the German language, *Schutzhund* translates to "protection dog." Many of the working dogs of Germany, the Boxer, Doberman Pinscher, Rottweiler and German Shepherd Dog, are trained in Schutzhund. Developed at the turn of the 20th century, Schutzhund includes not only protection training but also tracking and obedience. One of the principles of Schutzhund is that dogs must bark before they bite, and they are taught to seize and hold an opponent without actually tearing his limbs apart. Protection training for dogs utilizes a sleeve that the dog is taught to grasp and hold.

manns. Although Zunftig was in England only a short time before being sent to the US, he was able to sire the great Zulu, who was to become a profound influence on the British Boxer. Another fabulous German import from the Stockmanns was Frohlich von Dom, at the time considered the best import from Germany. From America, Dawson received excellent dogs from Mazelaine and Sirrah Crest, two of the most influential kennels in the States.

Panfield Serenade, owned by Elizabeth Montgomery-Somerfield, was the first bitch champion with The Kennel Club. Serenade was a granddaughter of Lustig. Pat Withers of the Witherford prefix also produced marvelous show dogs, including a line of four

Many prominent British kennels have imported Boxers from American breeders in an effort to give their dogs more flash and substance.

generations of champions. Her most famous dog is Int. Ch. Witherford's Hot Chestnut, who goes back to Collo von Dom, bred by Frau Stockmann. No matter which country you visit, the von Dom kennel influence is always present, a lasting tribute to the great Frau Stockmann.

The American influence on the Boxer in Britain can be traced to the country's respect for John P. Wagner, who visited England in the 1950s. Wagner was the proprietor of the famed Mazelaine Kennels, one of the largest Boxer establishments ever. The "flashiness" of the Boxer, ignited by the white blaze on the head, chest and feet, is associated with many famous American show dogs. The solid-colored fawn dogs, exemplary of the English Boxer tradition, were losing favor to the flashier American type. Eng. Ch. Seefeld's Picasso, bred by Pat Heath, is a fine example of a flashy Boxer who won grandly in the UK (acquiring some 24 Challenge Certificates).

Among other pioneers who paraded flashy Boxers was Charles Walker of the Lynpine Kennels, whose dogs trace back to Hot Chestnut (and therefore Frau Stockmann). Walker also introduced many great Dutch Boxers into his British bloodlines. The Newlaithe Boxers, owned by Christine and Patrick Beardsell, trace back to Frohlich von Dom.

The Boxer in the US possesses a stylish head, with elegant lines, flashy markings and good padding. This Jacquet dog well illustrates what's desired in the ideal Boxer head.

The next generation of Boxer champions. American breeders are among the most dedicated of Boxer fanciers around the world. Indeed, thanks to these folk, the 21st-century Boxer has become an "American breed."

This kennel has also imported some flashy American Boxers from the Jacquet Kennels.

BOXERS IN THE UNITED STATES

The Boxer, whose humble beginnings in Germany as a "mongrel" boar hunter, would rise to great fame around the world, not the least of which was in the US American breeders have had significant influence on the breed in many countries, with many imports sent to establish new bloodlines and to set the type of the "definitive show Boxer." The American dog scene has never recovered from the explosion of Bang Away in the 1950s. This likeable showman of a Boxer was featured on the cover of dog magazines and sports magazines alike! He paved the way for other show dogs to pursue astronomical heights in the ring. Although

ABC IN THE USA

The American Boxer Club, Inc., known as the ABC, has held a national specialty every year since 1936. The early years of the Boxer fancy in the US was dominated by great German imports, and the first winner of the specialty was Ch. Corso v. Uracher Wasserfall Se Sumbula, bred by Karl Walz of Germany. Entries at the first shows only drew around 50 dogs to compete; in time the show would attract over 400 Boxers.

Bang Away's record of 121 Bests in Show has been topped by many great show dogs in this day of modern travel and red-hot competition in the dog world, it has still not been topped by a Boxer! When Bang Away won the Westminster Kennel Club (WKC) show at Madison Square Garden in 1951, the breed was the top dog in registrations with the American Kennel Club. (Today the Boxer ranks in the top twenty, but rarely higher than ten.) Bang Away's Boxer predecessor as Westminster victor was Ch. Warlord of Mazelaine, bred by John P. Wagner and owned by Mr. and Mrs. Richard Kettles; his successor for the crown was Ch. Arriba's Prima Donna, bred by Theodore S. Fickes, DVM.

The American Boxer Club (ABC) was established in 1936, the same year that the Germans first organized their club. The ABC held its first specialty show that same year and it was won by Ch. Corso v. Uracher Wasserfall se Sumbula, bred by Karl Walz of Germany. Among the breed greats to win this Boxer showdown were Ch. Warlord of Mazelaine and Ch. Bang Away of Sirrah Crest, who both also won WKC; Ch. Baroque of Quality Hill; Ch. Treceder's Painted Lady; Ch. Salgray's Fashion Plate; Ch. Arriba's Prima Donna, also a WKC BIS winner; Ch. Scher-Khoun Shadrack of the famous Canadian kennel owned

BOXERS SERVING
The Boxer has been used in more areas of service to humankind than almost any other breed. Here are ten important areas that the breed has served:
1. Wartime and military work.
2. Police assistance and demonstrations.
3. Guides for the blind.
4. Hearing dogs for the deaf.
5. Arson and bomb detection.
6. Drug and substance detection.
7. Guard dogs for businesses and residences.
8. Search and rescue/avalanche and earthquake work.
9. Therapy dogs for hospitals.
10. Cancer detection.

by Ben de Boer; Ch. Wagner Wilverday Famous Amos, a four-time victor; and Ch. Kiebla's Tradition of Tu-Ro, a three-time victor (and three-time runner-up as Best of Opposite Sex). This list of greats fairly represents the best breeding in the US and the progeny of these great dogs produced magnificently in the States and elsewhere.

While Best of Breed at the national specialty is the most talked about ABC award in the fancy, the parent club also presents an annual award for Breeder of the Year and Kennel Finishing the Most Champions. Long-time breeder, Richard

The "definitive show Boxer" rules the conformation rings in the US.

Tomita accepted both of these awards for many consecutive years for the Jacquet Kennels, which are located in Oakland, New Jersey. Mr. Tomita has bred or co-bred over 200 American Kennel Club champions, including a handful of Best in Show winners, in addition to hundreds of international champions. Since its inception in 1971, the Jacquet Kennel family, including the many friends who have begun kennels with Jacquet stock, grows every year to include newcomers to the dog fancy plus many proud pet owners. Among the top show dogs and producers over the past three decades are: Ch. Happy Ours Fortune de Jacquet, who produced 35 AKC champions and over 60 international champions; Ch. Jacquet's Garnier; BIS Ch. Jacquet's Fleur de Lys, who produced three BIS sons in Ch. Kojak Von San Semo, Ch. Arrow's Sky High and Int. Ch. Jacquet's Urko; Int. Ch. Novarese; Ch. Jacquet's Bravo of Goldfield; Ch. Jacquet's Cambridge Fortune; Ch. Jacquet Jacquet's Agassiz; and so many others.

THE BOXER IN CANADA AND BEYOND

The Boxer in Canada was first recognized in 1934, and the first registered dog was Anthony Adverse of Barmere, owned by Marion Young (Breed), who purchased Sigurd von

Dom from Frau Stockmann. The American dog scene has always had great impact on the Canadian dog world, given the size of the US, its proximity and the open border between the two nations. Among the pioneer Canadian kennels, there are Quality, Allison, Blossomlea, Haviland and Malabar. The Boxer Club of Canada was formed in 1947, after the first club, the Western Boxer Club, disbanded the previous year. Among the nation's most famous Boxers is Int. Ch. Millan's Fashion Hint, out of Salgray bloodlines, who sired over 100 champions, including his world-renowned son Int. Ch. Scher-Khoun's Shadrack, also the sire of over 100 champions. Fashion Hint was bred and owned by Michael Millan. Among the top-producing kennels in Canada, there are Ajay, Bellcrest, Blossomlea, Chardepado, Diamondaire, Fisher, Gaylord, Glencotta, Golden Haze, Haviland, Jaegerhouse, Memorylane, Mephisto, Millan, Pinepath, Rodonna, Scher-Khoun, Shadowdale, Starview, Trimanor and Verwood, each of which has produced no fewer than 20 champions. Leading this prestigious pack is Haviland, which has produced about three times more than any other, totaling over 150 champions.

In Holland, the Boxer scene is lead off by Piet van Melis, whose observations about England and

The world's first long-tailed champion Boxer, Norwegian Ch. Boxerhavens Born for Adventure, is owned by Jorunn Selland. It seems quite unusual to see a Boxer with a natural tail.

the Continent are valuable: "In England, there is far less difference between the dogs because judges and breeders are looking more for the overall quality of the dog. In European countries, the head of the Boxer is of the highest importance, then comes the body, and movement is the last to be looked at." Despite Germany's stronghold on the Boxer breed, Holland has produced many excellent dogs, not the least of which is Mr. van Melis's Int. Ch. Casper van Worikben.

Despite the Germans' influence and predominance in the European Boxer world, the extremely independent Dutchmen

Indian Ch. Aryanoush's Vendetta was the Dog of the Year (All Breeds) and the Top Boxer in India. Owned by N. Adil Mirza.

Norwegian Ch. Astovega Opuntia, owned by Cecille Strømstad and Henning Lund.

Impala v. Okeler Forst, SchH. 1, AD, a Best in Show winner owned by Ralf Brinkmann, Germany, holds the title of World One Year Old Champion.

Tenor de Loermo, owned by Ernesto Molins and Juan Barcelo in Valencia, Spain, earned the title of the World Champion European Young Dog.

Indian Ch. Canara Coast Alaska, owned by Nita Dhar, Delhi, India, produced five champion offspring.

wanted little to do with the Germans after World War II and they discontinued use of the German lines. Over the years, the Dutch developed a distinctive Boxer that is heavy, strong and round, short-coated, with a superb head, not too short, and proportionate to the body.

In Germany, the Boxer must pass difficult tests in order to be considered a champion. These tests concern health, type and character. The first is an elementary test known as ZVP (which is very short for *Zuchtveranlangungsprufung*), which includes a check for "normal" or better hips. Additionally, a dog must pass three levels of Schutzhund tests and three levels of the IPO *(International Program d'Obeissance)*, and the test called *Ankorung*, a difficult test for type, quality and character, which is repeated every two years. German pedigrees list the results of these tests so that breeders can thoroughly and effectively evaluate the ancestry of the dogs (in terms of character, type and health). Unlike in the US and England, where a pedigree merely lists the names of the dogs in the ancestry (and whether or not they were champions), pedigrees in Germany give breeders insight into all the areas of importance to determine whether or not to breed to a certain dog. Fortunately for the international Boxer scene, more and more kennel clubs are encouraging this type of documentation on pedigrees.

The first American Boxer to be imported into Japan was sent in 1957 from the Mazelaine kennels, who was followed shortly by Ch. Canzonet's Minute-Minder, whose progeny dominated Japan in the 1960s. The American influence on Japan can hardly be overstated. Mazelaine sold some of their best dogs to Japan, including two ABC Best in Show winners. One of the most prominent Japanese Boxer breeders, Dr. Hideaki Nakazawa, also a popular judge in the US, has imported many great Boxers from the States, including Int. Ch.

The Scandinavian Norwegian Swedish Ch. Larun Your Choice was bred from top dogs in Norway and Finland.

Jacquet's Urko from the Jacquet kennel. Three other Jacquet Boxers followed, including the world-renowned Int. Ch. Novarese, and the Jacquet-style dog—strong, flashy, dramatic—began to dominate Japan. The Jacquet Boxers have "invaded" many other countries other than Japan, though given Mr. Tomita's Japanese ancestry, it's no wonder Jacquet has so generously shared dogs with his parents' homeland.

Among the other countries that Jacquet has influenced are Argentina, Australia, Brazil, Canada, India, Japan, the Philippines, Taiwan and Mexico. In *The World of the Boxer*, Mr. Tomita modestly pens, "I am happy to see Jacquet has helped to build the foundation for many lines and kennels throughout the world...I am grateful to the devoted Boxer fanciers and breeders who have guided me with their knowledge or their strong lines that they have produced so that I was able to further this wondrous world of the Boxer."

One of the most gorgeous Boxer heads in the world is held proud by the famous Spanish Ch. Janos de Loermo of Lynpine.

Although there have been hundreds of champions bred at Jacquet Boxers, not one of them compares to Jacquet's Holden, the beloved house pet of Bill Scolnik and breeder Rick Tomita.

Characteristics of the Boxer

IS THE BOXER THE RIGHT DOG FOR YOU?

Let's face it. Our Boxer today has very little to do with the bull-biting matadors of yesteryear. This author is certain that your reason for considering a Boxer is not to hold a hog down while you tie and spit it. Although it's fascinating to learn about the origins of our beloved Boxer, few of us today can relate to those butcher-dog legends. We can imagine, however, that the dog used to pin a wild boar to the forest floor needed courage, stamina and determination. These are three desirable qualities for a protection dog, which the Boxer delivers today with real style. I am not certain that the breed's original function required very much intelligence on the part of the dogs. It doesn't seem that an overly intelligent animal could fancy the gory, mindless work of the early Boxers. Nonetheless, the breed today has overcome this primitive mentality and is a resourceful, intelligent dog.

There are many endearing qualities that characterize the Boxer breed. He is sweet, good-humored, family-oriented, train-

Prospective owners selecting their house pet. By definition, the Boxer is sweet and family-oriented, thriving on the attention of people.

able and adaptable. The temperament of the Boxer cannot be compromised. Of all the working dogs, the Boxer stands out for the sweetness of his character. A mean Boxer is an oxymoron: no such animal should exist. Boxers are people dogs, devoutly attached to their families and protective of them. Today's Boxer is indeed a stylish companion dog as well as a guardian. This is a handsome dog who cuts a unique silhouette in dogdom. Standing proudly in the center ring at a dog show or in your doorway or backyard, the Boxer impresses all those who rest eyes upon him.

Within a family a Boxer thrives best. He is gentle with children, respectful of the elderly and obedient to each family member. Boxers recognize friends instinctively. Unlike less discriminating dogs, such as the Golden Retriever and Beagle, the Boxer does not accept everyone as his best friend. When your Boxer backs away from an individual or growls, he is telling you that there is something not quite right in the air. Boxers are tremendously good character judges. I have heard of more than one married couple who considered separating because the new Boxer decided

Do dogs get any cuter than this one? If you fall in love with a Boxer puppy, your expressions of attachment are a healthy part of dog-human bonding.

one or the other wasn't "up to snuff." Perhaps that's taking the Boxer's instincts too far—they are instinctive, not psychic!

To say that the Boxer is trainable is not to say that he is easily trained. A dedicated owner, who understands the way a Boxer thinks, will have very few problems training the Boxer. Unlike his ancestors, Boxers tend to ask "why" before they execute a command—especially before they execute a command four or five times simultaneously. Boxers tend to be too smart for their own good. This author has never read any legendary account of a medieval Boxer that refused to grab its fifteenth boar by the nose. Today's more-modern-thinking Boxers need a bit more prodding to execute obedience work. That there are hundreds of obedience-titled Boxers around us, not to mention highly trained service dogs, police dogs and military dogs, speaks well for the trainability of the Boxer. All these occupations also convince one of the adaptability of the Boxer, able to live in practically any situation with a family, a couple or just an individual. Since Boxers are so people-oriented, they care very little about their living environment. A Boxer can dwell contentedly in an apartment with a terrace, as long as he gets attention and adequate exercise. Similarly, the Boxer is content on a

grand estate with a large fenced-in property. He will guard both homes, and his owners, with his whole spirit and his whole heart.

Every Boxer's favorite holiday is Valentine's Day! Not just because this winter holiday is a great cause to warm up, but because it's about love and kissing. Boxers are great kissers—just ask a Boxer owner! Many breeders will confess that the Boxer is all

Boxers are famous for the ability to judge character. If they love you, they show it!

Though Boxers are rarely trained as water dogs, many of them do have an attraction to water.

THE LOVE OF A BOXER

You have never known love like the love of a Boxer. While the love of dogs is well known, the Boxer goes beyond the bounds of an owner's expectations. In a recent book by Jeffrey Moussaieff Masson, *Dogs Never Lie About Love*, he quotes Fritz von Unruh: "The dog is the only being that loves you more than you love yourself." I would bet that Fritz was a Boxer owner! Perhaps it is this love of humankind that has inspired the greater intelligence of our Boxers, the sweetness of temperament and the total trustworthiness of the Boxer breed. It is completely in harmony with modern-day thinking that such emotion could generate critical qualities in our companion animals.

bark. Once you get close to a group of vociferous Boxers, spewing and spitting as they announce their warning, they will lick you to death! That's not to suggest that the Boxer is incapable of defending his home. I have been astonished (repeatedly) every time one of my sweet loving Boxers suddenly turned bold and fearless at the sound of something threatening or ominous. Despite all the kissing and cooing, the Boxer is still a fearless guard dog. But still in all, he's more of a lover than a fighter!

Many people contend that the Boxer is a breed that you keep for life. Many of today's Boxer owners grew up with a Boxer or remember being strongly imprinted upon by a Boxer (perhaps an uncle or neighbor had an outstanding dog). Having grown up with a Boxer often convinces adults to share a Boxer with their own children. On the other hand, many households without children adopt Boxers because they are described as being as intelligent as a seven-year-old child, and surely more obedient! Then there are those "grown-up" parents, whose children have moved out of the household, who adopt a Boxer for their golden years. As Boxer people will reveal, a home is not a home without a Boxer.

The Boxer has proven its worth to humankind by performing in various service capacities. In addition to its role in the military, the Boxer has donned a badge as a police dog, assisting the legal forces of many nations. In homes, the Boxer's steady temperament and affinity for the human touch have made the breed a superior choice for therapy dogs. Whether the Boxer's ears drop naturally or stand erect, it is first and foremost a "hearing" dog. The AKC standard describes the Boxer as a "'hearing' guard dog," thus also making him a definitive choice for the deaf. Other physically challenged individuals rely on Boxers as well, including those confined to a wheelchair and the blind, for whom the Boxer serves as a Seeing Eye™ dog or guide dog. Not only does the Boxer offer his ears and eyes to humankind, he also offers his nose! As a search and rescue dog, the Boxer has assisted rescue workers in emergencies, such as earthquakes and avalanches. The Boxer is able to "sniff" out lost individuals buried under knee-deep snow, rock or rubble.

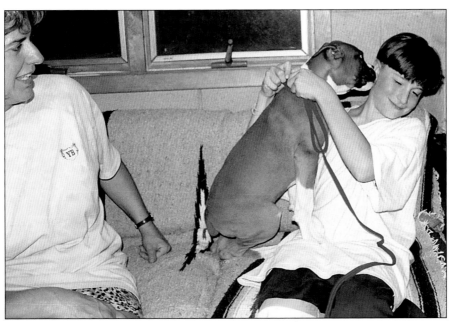

Boxers are kissers; they are lovers not fighters!

The standard describes the beauty of the head as the harmonious proportion of the muzzle and skull. This Jacquet champion illustrates the desired chiseled head that imparts the breed's unique stamp.

Breed Standard for the Boxer

Definition: A standard is a written description of what the ideal representative of a breed should look and act like.

A standard is drafted by a breed club, like the American Boxer Club or the German Boxer Club, and then submitted for acceptance to the national kennel club. The American Kennel Club controls all standards for the US Breeders and other experts usually convene to put the ineffable perfect dog into words. Composing such a word picture is fraught with difficulty and dissension, since words are prone to interpretation and the meaning of words vary. For instance, if a dog's muzzle is described as "broad and deep," just how broad and how deep should the perfect muzzle be? What is in balance to one viewer is totally out of balance to the next. Thus, breeders could never agree on the perfect dog even if it walked into the show ring! Nonetheless, the breed standard is the best measuring stick available for determining which Boxers are excellent and which are below-average. The American Boxer standard, as accepted by the American Kennel Club, has many sections that are very specific. Study the Head and Skull section carefully. There is no doubt that fanciers revere the Boxer's head, and the detail set forth in the standard on the head does not leave too much room for poor interpretation. The standard is used by judges in the show ring, just as breeders use the standard to decide which dogs are worth breeding and which dogs are not.

The standard included here is approved by the American Kennel Club, the leading dog-governing body of the US. It was approved by the AKC on March 14, 1989.

How will your new puppy "stack" up against the standard? Whether you are purchasing a pet dog or a show dog, you still want a Boxer who looks and acts like the breed you've so carefully chosen.

THE AMERICAN KENNEL CLUB STANDARD FOR THE BOXER

General Appearance: The ideal Boxer is a medium-sized, square built dog of good substance with short back, strong limbs, and short, tight-fitting coat. His well developed muscles are clean, hard and appear smooth under taut skin. His movements denote energy. The gait is firm, yet elastic, the stride free and ground-covering, the carriage proud. Developed to serve as guard, working and companion dog, he combines strength and agility with elegance and style. His expression is alert and temperament steadfast and tractable.

The chiseled head imparts to the Boxer a unique individual stamp. It must be in correct proportion to the body. The broad, blunt muzzle is the distinctive feature, and great value is placed upon its being of proper form and balance with the skull.

In judging the Boxer, first consideration is given to general appearance to which attractive color and arresting style contribute. Next is overall balance with special attention devoted to the head, after which the individual body components are examined for their correct construction, and efficiency of gait is evaluated.

Size, Proportion, Substance: *Height*—Adult males 22.5 to 25 inches; females 21 to 23.5 inches at the withers, preferably, males should not be under the minimum nor females over the maximum: however, proper balance and quality in the individual should be of primary importance since there is no size disqualification. *Proportion*—The body in profile is of square proportion in that a horizontal line from the front of the forechest to the rear projection of the upper thigh should equal the length of a vertical line dropped from the top of the withers to the ground. *Substance*—Sturdy with balanced musculature. Males larger boned than their female counterparts.

Head: The beauty of the head depends upon harmonious proportion of muzzle to skull. The blunt muzzle is one-third the length of the head from the occiput to the tip of the nose, and two-thirds the width of the skull. The head should be clean, not showing deep wrinkles (wet). Wrinkles typically appear upon the forehead when ears are erect, and folds are always present from the lower edge of the stop running downward on both sides of the muzzle. *Expression*—Intelligent and alert. *Eyes*—Dark brown in color, not too small, too protruding or too deep-set. Their mood-mirroring character, combined with the wrinkling of the forehead, gives the Boxer head its unique quality of expressiveness. *Ears*—Set at the highest points of the sides of the skull are cropped, cut rather long and tapering, raised when alert. *Skull*—The top of the skull is slightly arched, not rounded, flat nor noticeably broad, with the occiput not overly pronounced. The forehead shows a slight indentation between the eyes and forms a distinct stop with the topline of the muzzle. The cheeks should be relatively flat and not bulge (cheekiness), maintaining the clean lines of the skull and should taper into the muzzle in a slight, graceful curve. *Muzzle*—The muzzle, proportionately developed in length, width and depth, has a shape influenced first through the formation of both jawbones, second through the placement of the teeth, and third through the texture of the lips.

The top of the muzzle should not slant down (downfaced), nor should it be concave (dishfaced); however, the tip of the nose should lie slightly higher than the root of the muzzle. The nose should be broad and black.

The upper jaw is broad where attached to the skull and maintains this breadth except for a very slight tapering to the front. The lips, which complete the formation of the muzzle, should meet evenly in front. The upper lip is thick and padded, filling out the frontal space created by the projection of the lower jaw, and laterally is supported by the

canines of the lower jaw. Therefore, these canines must stand far apart and be of good length so that the front surface of the muzzle is broad and squarish and, when viewed from the side, shows moderate layback. The chin should be perceptible from the side as well as from the front. *Bite*—The Boxer bite is undershot; the lower jaw protrudes beyond the upper and curves slightly upward. The incisor teeth of the lower jaw are in a straight line, with the canines preferably up front in the same line to give the jaw the greatest possible width. The upper line of incisors is

In the show ring, the judge compares each competing Boxer against the breed standard. The winner of the class is the dog that the judge feels is closest to the standard.

slightly convex with the corner upper incisors fitting snugly back of the lower canine teeth on each side. *Faults*—Skull too broad. Cheekiness. Wrinkling too deep (wet) or lacking (dry). Excessive flews. Muzzle too light for skull. Too pointed a bite (snipy), too undershot, teeth or tongue showing when mouth closed. Eyes noticeably lighter than ground color of coat.

Neck, Topline, Body: *Neck*—Round, of ample length, muscular and clean without excessive hanging skin (dewlap). The neck has a distinctly marked nape with an elegant arch blending smoothly into the withers. *Topline*—Smooth, firm and slightly sloping. *Body*—The chest is of fair width, and the forechest well defined and visible from the side. The brisket is deep, reaching down to the elbows; the depth of the body at the lowest point of the brisket equals half the height of the dog at the withers. The ribs, extending far to the rear, are well arched but not barrel shaped.

The back is short, straight and muscular and firmly connects the withers to the hindquarters. The loins are short and muscular. The lower stomach line is slightly tucked up, blending into a graceful curve to the rear. The croup is slightly sloped, flat and broad. Tail is set high, docked and carried upward. Pelvis long and in

females especially broad. *Faults*—Short heavy neck. Chest too broad, too narrow or hanging between shoulders. Lack of forechest. Hanging stomach. Slab-sided rib cage. Long or narrow loin, weak union with croup. Falling off of croup. Higher in rear than in front.

Forequarters: The shoulders are long and sloping, close-lying, and not excessively covered with muscle (loaded). The upper arm is long, approaching a right angle to the shoulder blade. The elbows should not press too closely to the chest wall nor stand off visibly from it.

The forelegs are long, straight and firmly muscled and when viewed from the front, stand parallel to each other. The pastern is strong and distinct, slightly slanting, but standing almost perpendicular to the ground. The dewclaws may be removed. Feet should be compact, turning neither in nor out, with well arched toes. *Faults*—Loose or loaded shoulders. Tied in or bowed out elbows.

Hindquarters: The hindquarters are strongly muscled with angulation in balance with that of the forequarters. The thighs are broad and curved, the breech musculature hard and strongly developed. Upper and lower thigh long. Leg well angulated at the stifle with a clearly defined, well "let down"

The muzzle of the Boxer is shaped through the bone formation, placement of the teeth and texture of the lips.

hock joint. Viewed from behind, the hind legs should be straight with hock joints leaning neither in nor out. From the side, the leg below the hock (metatarsus) should be almost perpendicular to the ground, with a slight slope to the rear permissible. The metatarsus should be short, clean and strong. The Boxer has no rear dewclaws. *Faults*—Steep or over-angulated hindquarters. Light thighs or overdeveloped hams. Over-angulated (sickle) hocks. Hindquarters too far under or too far behind.

Coat: Short, shiny, lying smooth and tight to the body.

Color: The colors are fawn and brindle. Fawn shades vary from light tan to mahogany. The brindle ranges from sparse, but clearly defined black stripes on a fawn background, to such a heavy concentration of black striping that the essential fawn background color barely, although clearly, shows through (which may create the appearance of "reverse brindling").

White markings should be of such distribution as to enhance the dog's appearance, but may not exceed one-third of the entire coat. They are not desirable on the flanks or on the back of the torso proper. On the face, white may replace part of the otherwise essential black mask and may extend in an upward path between the eyes, but it must not be excessive, so as to detract from true Boxer expression. *Faults*—Unattractive or misplaced white markings. *Disqualifications*—Boxers that are any color other than fawn or brindle. Boxers with a total of white markings exceeding one-third of the entire coat.

Gait: Viewed from the side, proper front and rear angulation is manifested in a smoothly efficient, level-backed, ground covering stride with powerful drive emanating from a freely operating rear. Although the front legs do not contribute impelling power, adequate "reach" should be evident to prevent interference, overlap or "sidewinding" (crabbing). Viewed from the front, the shoulders should remain trim and the elbows not flare out. The legs are parallel until gaiting narrows the track in proportion to increasing speed, then the legs come in under the body but should never cross. The line from the shoulder down through the leg should remain straight although not necessarily perpendicular to the ground. Viewed from the rear, a Boxer's rump should not roll. The hind feet should "dig in" and track relatively true with the front. Again, as speed increases, the normally broad rear track will become narrower. *Faults*—Stilted or inefficient gait. Lack of smoothness.

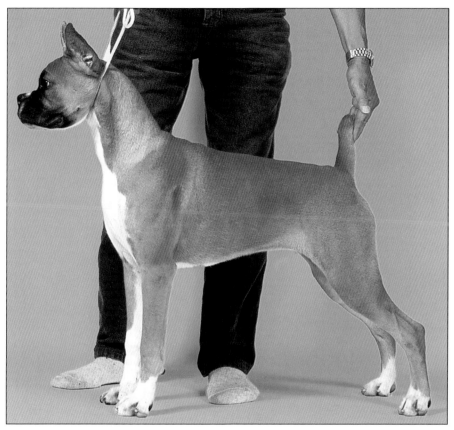

The neck of the Boxer should smoothly arch, with a distinct nape, blending into the withers, while the topline should be smooth, firm and slightly sloping.

Character and Temperament: These are of paramount importance in the Boxer. Instinctively a "hearing" guard dog, his bearing is alert, dignified and self-assured. In the show ring, his behavior should exhibit constrained animation. With family and friends, his temperament is fundamentally playful, yet patient and stoical with children. Deliberate and wary with strangers, he will exhibit curiosity but, most importantly, fearless courage if threatened. However, he responds promptly to friendly overtures honestly rendered. His intelligence, loyal affection and tractability to discipline make him a highly desirable companion. *Faults*—Lack of dignity and alertness. Shyness.

Disqualifications: Boxers that are any color other than fawn or brindle. Boxers with a total of white markings exceeding one-third of the entire coat.

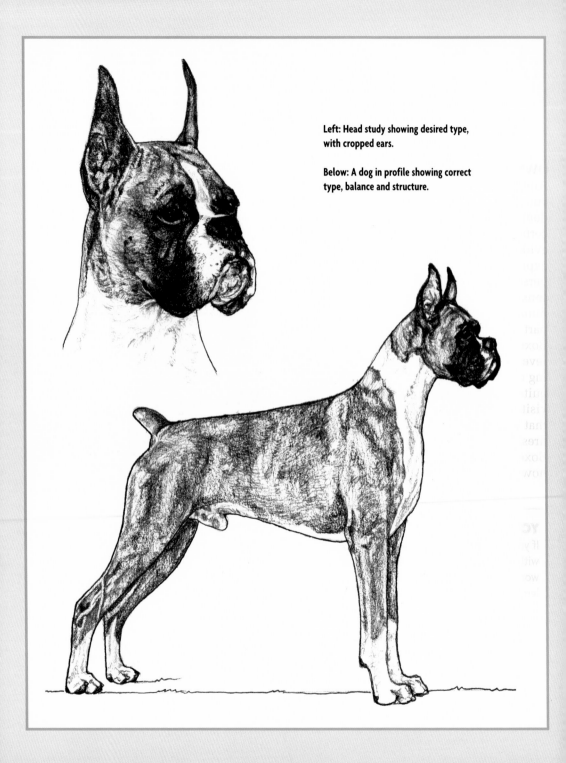

Left: Head study showing desired type, with cropped ears.

Below: A dog in profile showing correct type, balance and structure.

Your Puppy Boxer

OWNER CONSIDERATIONS

Any admirer of the Boxer can tell you that he is a proud and confident dog. This "pure-bred" certainty goes without saying—it's evident in the Boxer's carriage, his expression and his distinctive personality. But a Boxer is also a sensitive creature that depends on human interaction. This is a vital part of what makes a Boxer a Boxer. Boxers thrive on people, revealing in the licking and kissing of their families, and often quite eager to "taste" any willing visitor. If you are looking for a dog that will sit handsomely by the fireside and never bother you, the Boxer is not the dog for you. If, however, you are willing to

A proper breeder would not sell a puppy to people who would not or could not care for the Boxer puppy in a safe and humane manner.

devote the time and attention to a Boxer that he rightly deserves, this is a breed for you for life!

Although the reader of these pages is more likely interested in finding a companionable family animal than a show champion, there remain many serious factors governing your choice. A primary consideration is time, not only the time of the animal's allotted lifespan, which is over ten years, but also the time required for the owner to exercise and care for the creature. If you are not committed to the welfare and whole existence of this energetic, purposeful animal; if, in the simplest, most basic example, you are not willing to walk your dog daily, despite the weather, do not choose a Boxer as a companion.

Space is another important

YOUR SCHEDULE ...

If you lead an erratic, unpredictable life, with daily or weekly changes in your work requirements, consider the problems of owning a puppy. The new puppy has to be fed regularly, socialized (loved, petted, handled, introduced to other people) and, most importantly, allowed to go outdoors for house-training. As the dog gets older, he can be more tolerant of deviations in his feeding and relief schedule.

FAMILY TIES

If you have other pets in the home and/or interact often with the pets of friends and other family members, your pup will respond to those pets in much the same manner as you do. It is only when you show fear or resentment toward another animal that he will act fearful or unfriendly.

Boxers are prone to certain genetic diseases. Buy a healthy puppy and have him examined by a vet as soon as you take him home.

consideration. The Boxer in early puppyhood may be well accommodated in a corner of your kitchen but, after only six months when the dog is likely over 40 pounds, larger space certainly will be required. A yard with a fence is also a basic and reasonable expectation. Fortunately, most Boxers do not stray far from their properties (unless attracted by a strong-scented bitch). Unlike other breeds that tend to "escape" on a regular basis, the Boxer will not abandon his post. The fence is a convenient detail because it also keeps strangers from wandering upon your property and challenging your Boxer.

A Boxer is not an outdoor dog. He wants to be as close to you as possible. He is not appropriately "dressed" to spend all his days outside. He needs to be indoors with the family. A Boxer that is kept outdoors exclusively is a miserable dog. Don't subject your dog to such a life. Boxers do not tend to be independent and they want to follow you, spend time with you, sit with you, etc. Make sure that you want a Boxer in your home and in your life.

Remember too that Boxer puppies can be very inventive, that is to say, destructive. Unless you can supervise a puppy 24 hours per day, you must expect that he's going to investigate and taste your woodwork, furniture, cabinets, etc. You must be prepared (emotionally and financially) for such mishaps. Needless to say, proper training and a dash

Try to observe your prospective Boxer puppy with his dam. If the dam plays with the puppies, you can take delight in knowing that your pup will likely have an inherited friendly attitude.

of discipline are all it takes to correct such problems. If you are extremely fussy about your house and cannot tolerate muddy paws and slobbery jowls, go for a guppy or parakeet and spare a Boxer the disappointment.

Likewise, the potential owner must consider that a dog impedes upon his freedom! You can no longer escape for a long weekend without preparing for your Boxer's accommodations. Perhaps you will choose a vacation that is suitable for a dog to come along, but the Boxer must now figure into your planning. Once you have selected a Boxer, and you have bonded with him, you will realize that you have found the ideal companion, one who accepts you for all your faults and appreciates

every little thing you do for him! The Boxer's life expectancy is a sure ten years, perhaps even a few years longer. Since 10 to 12 years is a long expanse of time, you must commit to keeping the Boxer for his whole life. Many Boxers are successfully rehomed (placed in second homes) through rescue

It is difficult to judge a puppy's personality until he is at least four weeks old.

White puppies in a litter should not alarm the potential pet buyer. These puppies are throwbacks to ancestors of the original Boxer, which is a man-made breed from several other dogs.

groups. Fortunately the Boxer's adaptability makes this unfortunate, heartbreaking situation more bearable. It's possible that you might want to consider adopting a Boxer from a rescue group. Since adopting an adult dog is almost always easier than starting from scratch (and bite) with a puppy, this is a sensible, viable option for many. If you would like to give a deserving Boxer a second chance, contact your local breed club or the AKC for the appropriate source.

ACQUIRING A BOXER PUPPY
Due to the popularity of the Boxer, there are many reputable breeders to choose from, and there are even more breeders to avoid. You should seek out the best Boxer that you can afford. There is no such thing as "just a pet dog" or a "pet-quality dog." You cannot afford to own a second-rate dog. Inferior quality in a pet only translates to high veterinary bills, wasted time and broken hearts! You are seeking a Boxer that looks and acts like a Boxer.

If you buy a Boxer puppy, you must accept the responsibilities of ownership for at least ten years. Boxers usually live for over a decade.

You want your neighbors to admire your canine charge and tell you how handsome he is. If the appearance of the dog doesn't matter, why get a Boxer? It's not that simple. You want a hand-some Boxer that is the picture of good health: a pedigree that indicates his parents have normal or better hips, no history of cancers or the like in their backgrounds and good eyes. Since the Boxer is prone to a number of genetic problems, you want the healthiest dog you can find. You're not merely investing money in this purchase—you're investing your heart and your family! What could be more costly than that? If the breeder is trying to pitch a "pet-quality puppy" at you, tell him that you want the best puppy he has. While the conformation of the dog isn't a primary consideration for a pet person, all of the other important factors that breeders emphasize are. Reread the temperament and character portion of the breed standard: is

there a single quality listed there that doesn't appeal to you?

Be aware that the novice breeders who advertise at attractive prices in the local newspapers are probably kind enough towards their dogs, but often do not have the expertise or facilities required to raise these dogs properly. These pet puppies are frequently badly weaned and left with the mother too long without the supplemental feeding required by this fast-growing breed. This lack of proper feeding can cause indigestion, rickets, weak bones, poor teeth and other problems. Veterinary bills may soon distort initial savings into financial or, worse, emotional loss. Inquire about inoculations and when the puppy was last dosed for worms. Check the ears for signs of debris or irritation, indicating the presence of mites.

Color is a matter of personal choice, but whether you prefer a bright fawn Boxer with flashy white markings or a brindle dog, your puppy should have a dark nose and, preferably, dark toenails. This is a consideration of pigmentation, which should not be confused with color. Color in Boxers generally becomes lighter, so it is wise to choose a puppy with deep rich pigmentation and as much black as possible. By six to ten weeks of age, the Boxer's nose should be well pigmented and broad. You do not want a

REGULAR PLAY SESSIONS

Your Boxer should have regular play and exercise sessions when he is with you or a family member. Exercise for a very young puppy can consist of a short walk around the house or yard. Playing can include fetching games with a large ball or an old sock with a knot tied in the middle. (All puppies teethe and need soft things upon which to chew.) Remember to restrict play periods to indoors within his living area (the family room, for example) until he is completely house-trained.

Boxer puppy with a narrow nose, since his muzzle will likely not develop to the desired broadness. In selecting a fawn-colored dog, seek a deep red coloration, especially down the back and head; in a brindle dog, look for distinctive

This Boxer puppy's color is not acceptable for a show dog, but as a pet dog the color is enchanting.

should have some wrinkles, which will disappear as the dog matures. Check that the puppy's lower jaw is as wide as possible, ideal for incoming adult teeth. Never sacrifice overall balance and harmony for a fabulous head. Judges will view the whole picture, not just the dog's head.

Note the way your choice moves. The Boxer, even in puppyhood, should show clean

herringbone striations against a deep red background. For the flashy look, white markings should be present on the chest, legs and forehead and muzzle.

In show dogs, breeders seek out deep pigmentation complemented by white markings on the head, legs and chest. Dark eyes are best, and Boxer pups tend to have bluish eyes that darken as they age. Look for expression in your puppy's eyes, as this is a good sign of intelligence. Boxers often show the haw of the eye, one or both of which may be white; this adds to the Boxer expression. Since the Boxer is a "head breed," you want a puppy that makes a pleasing impression. The Boxer puppy's muzzle should be broad and deep; this is important for the expression of the dog as an adult. The puppy's head

BOY OR GIRL?

An important consideration to be discussed is the sex of your puppy. For a family companion, a bitch may be the better choice, considering the female's inbred concern for all young creatures and her accompanying tolerance and patience. It is always advisable to spay a pet bitch, which may guarantee her a longer life.

movement with no tendency to stumble or drag the hind feet. Boxers tend to be awkward in their puppy months, so do not confuse this immature lack of coordination with a structural defect. It's best to take along an experienced Boxer person if you are concerned about the structure of the puppy. This tends to be a show-dog concern more than a pet concern, though we all want Boxers that can move easily and effortlessly. In evaluating the structure of your pup, consider that the topline (along his back) should be as straight as possible, with the shoulders sloping and the back short. Avoid toplines that "roach" toward the center (rise noticeably), weak rear quarters, poor feet and, of course, shy or spooky temperaments.

The puppy's bite should be somewhat undershot, meaning the lower jaw protrudes further than the upper jaw. Look for a

PEDIGREE VS. REGISTRATION CERTIFICATE

Too often new owners are confused between these two important documents. Your puppy's pedigree, essentially a family tree, is a written record of a dog's genealogy of three generations or more. The pedigree will show you the names as well as performance titles of all the dogs in your pup's background. Your breeder must provide you with a registration application, with his part properly filled out. You must complete the application and send it to the AKC with the proper fee. Every puppy must come from a litter that has been AKC-registered by the breeder, born in the US and from sire and dam that are also registered with the AKC.

The seller must provide you with complete records to identify the puppy. The AKC requires that the seller provide the buyer with the following: breed; sex, color and markings; date of birth; litter number (when available); names and registration numbers of the parents; breeder's name; and date sold or delivered.

Boxer puppies should be playful, lively and alert. They should be outgoing and neither shy nor frightened.

lower jaw line that is as wide as possible. Be sure that the tongue doesn't stick out when the puppy closes his mouth. The bite is important for show dogs as well as pet dogs. Although your pet puppy won't be disqualified at the dinner table for an incorrect bite, he may not be able to eat and breathe comfortably throughout his life.

When you bring your Boxer puppy home, he should have a crate or bed...someplace to which he can retreat for a nap.

COMMITMENT OF OWNERSHIP

After considering all of these factors, you have most likely already made some very important decisions about selecting your puppy. You have chosen the Boxer, which means that you have decided which characteristics you want in a dog and what type of dog will best fit into your family and lifestyle. If you have selected a breeder, you have gone a step further—you have done your research and found a responsible, conscientious person who breeds quality Boxers and who should be a reliable source of help as you and your puppy adjust to life together. If you have observed a litter in action, you have obtained a firsthand look at the dynamics of a puppy "pack" and, thus, you have gotten to learn about each pup's individual personality— perhaps you have even found one that particularly appeals to you.

However, even if you have not yet found the Boxer puppy of your dreams, observing pups will help you learn to recognize certain behavior and to determine what a pup's behavior indicates about his temperament. You will be able to pick out which pups are the leaders, which ones are less outgoing, which ones are confident, which ones are shy, playful, friendly, aggressive, etc. Equally as important, you will learn to recognize what a healthy pup should look and act like. All of these things will help you in your search, and when you find

ARE YOU PREPARED?

Unfortunately, when a puppy is bought by someone who does not take into consideration the time and attention that dog ownership requires, it is the puppy who suffers when he is either abandoned or placed in a shelter by a frustrated owner. So all of the "homework" you do in preparation for your pup's arrival will benefit you both. The more informed you are, the more you will know what to expect and the better equipped you will be to handle the ups and downs of raising a puppy. Hopefully, everyone in the household is willing to do his part in raising and caring for the pup. The anticipation of owning a dog often brings a lot of promises from excited family members: "I will walk him every day," "I will feed him," "I will house-train him," etc., but these things take time and effort, and promises can easily be forgotten once the novelty of the new pet has worn off.

PET INSURANCE

Just like you can insure your car, your house and your own health, you likewise can insure your dog's health. Investigate a pet insurance policy by talking to your vet. Depending on the age of your dog, the breed and the kind of coverage you desire, your policy can be very affordable. Most policies cover accidental injuries, poisoning and thousands of medical problems and illnesses, including cancers. Some carriers also offer routine care and immunization coverage.

the Boxer that was meant for you, you will know it!

Researching your breed, selecting a responsible breeder and observing as many pups as possible are all important steps on the way to dog ownership. It may seem like a lot of effort...and you have not even brought the pup home yet! Remember, though, you cannot be too careful when it comes to deciding on the type of dog you want and finding out about your prospective pup's background. Buying a puppy is not—or should not be—just another whimsical purchase. In fact, this is one instance in which you actually do get to choose your own family! But, you may be thinking, buying a puppy should be fun—it should not be so serious and so much work. If you keep in mind the thought that

your puppy is not a cuddly stuffed toy or decorative lawn ornament, but instead will become a real member of your family, you will realize that, while buying a puppy is a pleasurable and exciting endeavor, it is not something to be taken lightly. Relax...the fun will start when the pup comes home!

Always keep in mind that a puppy is nothing more than a baby in a furry disguise...a baby who is virtually helpless in a human world and who trusts his owner for fulfillment of his basic needs for survival. That goes beyond food, water and shelter; your pup needs care, protection, guidance and love. If you are not prepared to commit to this, then you are not prepared to own a dog.

"Wait a minute," you say. "How hard could this be? All of my neighbors own dogs and they seem to be doing just fine. Why should I have to worry about all of this?" Well, you should not worry about it; in fact, you will probably find that once your

Just yesterday your Boxer pup was playing, sleeping and eating with his siblings. The first day in your home is a completely new experience for your new charge.

Boxer pup gets used to his new home, he will fall into his place in the family quite naturally. But it never hurts to emphasize the commitment of dog ownership. With some time and patience, it is really not too difficult to raise a curious and exuberant Boxer pup to be a well-adjusted and well-mannered adult dog—a dog that could be your most loyal friend.

PREPARING PUPPY'S PLACE IN YOUR HOME

Researching your breed and finding a breeder are only two aspects of the "homework" you will have to do before bringing your Boxer puppy home. You will also have to prepare your home and family for the new addition. Much like you would prepare a nursery for a newborn baby, you will need to designate a place in your home that will be the puppy's own. How you prepare your home will depend on how much freedom the dog will be allowed: will he be confined to one room or a specific area in the house, or will he be allowed to roam as he pleases? Will he spend most of his time in the house? Will he have an outdoor house too? Whatever you decide, you must ensure that he has a place that he can "call his own" in your home.

When you bring your new puppy into your home, you are bringing him into what will become his home as well. Obviously, you did not buy a puppy so that he could take over your house, but in order for a puppy to grow into a stable, well-adjusted dog, he has to feel comfortable in his surroundings. Remember, he is leaving the warmth and security of his mother and littermates, plus the familiarity of the only place he has ever known, so it is important to make his transition as easy

It only takes a short time before your Boxer puppy becomes a well-mannered family member who will fit into your lifestyle and make himself comfortable in most situations.

as possible. By preparing a place in your home for the puppy, you are making him feel as welcome as possible in a strange new place. It should not take him long to get used to it, but the sudden shock of being transplanted is somewhat traumatic for a young pup. Imagine how a small child would feel in the same situation—that is how your puppy must be feeling. It is up to you to reassure him and to let him know, "Little guy, you are going to like it here!"

WHAT YOU SHOULD BUY

CRATE

To someone unfamiliar with the use of crates in dog training, it may seem like punishment to shut a dog in a crate; this is not the case at all. Crates are not cruel—crates have many humane and highly effective uses in dog care and training. For example, crate training is a very popular and very successful housebreaking method; a crate can keep your dog safe during travel; and, perhaps most importantly, a crate provides your dog with a place of his own in your home. It serves as a "doggie bedroom" of sorts—your Boxer can curl up in his crate when he wants to sleep or when he just needs a break. Many dogs sleep in their crates overnight. When lined with soft padding and with his favorite toy inside, a crate becomes a cozy pseudo-den for your dog. Like his ancestors, he too will seek out the comfort and retreat of a den—you just happen to be providing him with something a little more luxurious than leaves and twigs lining a dirty ditch.

You will have to be prepared for bringing a new puppy home. Keep in mind that your puppy has always been surrounded with other Boxers, other puppies and even other people. You have become the substitute "pack." Are you ready for this?

THE COCOA WARS

Chocolate contains the chemical thebromine, which is poisonous to dogs, although "chocolates" especially made for dogs are safe (as they don't actually contain chocolate) but not recommended. Any item that encourages your dog to enjoy the taste of cocoa should be discouraged. You should also exercise caution when using mulch in your garden. This frequently contains cocoa hulls, and dogs have been known to die from eating the mulch.

PHOTO COURTESY OF MIKKI PET PRODUCTS.

puppies forever—in fact, sometimes it seems as if they grow right before your eyes. A small-sized crate may be fine for a very young Boxer pup, but it will not do him much good for long! Unless you have the money and the inclination to buy a new crate every time your pup has a growth spurt, it is better to get one that will accommodate your dog both as a pup and at full size. A large crate of sufficient height will be necessary for a full-grown Boxer, as their approximate weight range is between 55 and 70 pounds.

BEDDING

A crate pad in the dog's crate will help the dog feel more at home. First, the bedding will take the

As far as purchasing a crate, the type that you buy is up to you. It will most likely be one of the two most popular types: wire or fiberglass. There are advantages and disadvantages to each type. For example, a wire crate is more open, allowing the air to flow through and affording the dog a view of what is going on around him. A fiberglass crate, however, is sturdier and more suitable as a travel crate since it provides more protection for the dog. The size of the crate is another thing to consider. Puppies do not stay

CRATE-TRAINING TIPS

During crate training, you should partition off the section of the crate in which the pup stays. If he is given too big an area, this will hinder your training efforts. Crate training is based on the fact that a dog does not like to soil his sleeping quarters, so it is ineffective to keep a pup in an area that is so big that he can eliminate in one end and get far enough away from it to sleep. Also, you want to make the crate den-like for the pup. Blankets and a favorite toy will make the crate cozy for the small pup; as he grows, you may want to evict some of his "roommates" to make more room. It will take some coaxing at first, but be patient. Given some time to get used to it, your pup will adapt to his new home-within-a-home quite nicely.

place of the leaves, twigs, etc., that the pup would use in the wild to make a den; the pup can make his own "burrow" in the crate. Although your pup is far removed from his den-making ancestors, the denning instinct is still a part of his genetic makeup. Second, until you bring your pup home, he has been sleeping amid the warmth of his mother and littermates, and while a pad is not the same as a warm, breathing body, it still provides heat and something with which to snuggle. You will want to wash your pup's bedding frequently in case he has an accident in his crate, and replace or remove any bedding that becomes ragged and starts to fall apart.

Toys

Toys are a must for dogs of all ages, especially for curious playful pups. Puppies are the "children" of the dog world, and what child does not love toys? Chew toys provide enjoyment to both dog and owner—your dog will enjoy playing with his favorite toys, while you will enjoy the fact that they distract him from your expensive shoes and leather sofa. Puppies love to chew; in fact, chewing is a physical need for

Not only are crates valuable for training, but dogs whose ears have been cropped, or who have undergone other surgical procedures, can be securely isolated for recuperation.

pups as they are teething, and everything looks appetizing! The full range of your possessions—from old rag to Oriental rug—are fair game in the eyes of a teething pup. Puppies are not all that discerning when it comes to finding something to literally "sink their teeth into"—everything tastes great!

Stuffed toys are another option; these are good to put in the dog's crate to give him some company. Be careful of these, as a pup can de-stuff one pretty quickly, and stay away from stuffed toys with small plastic eyes or parts that a pup could choke on. Similarly, squeaky toys are quite popular. There are dogs that will come running from anywhere in the house at the first sound from their favorite squeaky friend. However, if a pup de-stuffs

PHOTO COURTESY OF MIKKI PET PRODUCTS.

one of these, the small plastic squeaker inside can be dangerous if swallowed. Monitor the condition of your pup's toys carefully and get rid of any that have been chewed to the point of becoming potentially dangerous.

Be careful of natural bones, which have a tendency to splinter into sharp, dangerous pieces. Also be careful of rawhide, which after enough chewing can turn into pieces that are easy to swallow, and also watch out for the mushy mess it can turn into on your carpet.

purposes, the nylon leash is a good choice. As your pup grows up and gets used to walking on the leash, and can do it politely, you may want to purchase a flexible leash, which allows you either to extend the length to give the dog a broader area to explore or to pull in the leash when you want

LEASH

A nylon leash is probably the best option, as it is the most resistant to puppy teeth should your pup take a liking to chewing on his leash. Of course, this is a habit that should be nipped in the bud, but if your pup likes to chew on his leash he has a very slim chance of being able to chew through the strong nylon. Nylon leashes are also lightweight, which is good for a young Boxer who is just getting used to the idea of walking on a leash. For everyday walking and safety

---

CHEWING TIPS

Chewing goes hand in hand with nipping in the sense that a teething puppy is always looking for a way to soothe his aching gums. In this case, instead of chewing on you, he may have taken a liking to your favorite shoe or something else which he should not be chewing. Again, realize that this is a normal canine behavior that does not need to be discouraged, only redirected. Your pup just needs to be taught what is acceptable to chew on and what is off-limits. Consistently tell him "No!" when you catch him chewing on something forbidden and give him a chew toy.

Conversely, praise him when you catch him chewing on something appropriate. In this way, you are discouraging the inappropriate behavior and reinforcing the desired behavior. The puppy's chewing should stop after his adult teeth have come in, but an adult dog continues to chew for various reasons—perhaps because he is bored, needs to relieve tension or just likes to chew. That is why it is important to redirect his chewing when he is still young.

to keep him close. Of course there are special leashes for training purposes, and specially made leather harnesses for the working Boxer, but these are not necessary for routine walks. For the adult Boxer who tends to pull on the leash, you may want to purchase something stronger, like a thicker leather leash.

COLLAR

Your pup should get used to wearing a collar all the time since you will want to attach his ID tags to his collar. Also, the lead and collar go hand in hand—you have to attach the leash to something! A lightweight nylon collar will be a good choice; make sure that it fits snugly enough so that the pup

Pet shops usually carry an extensive range of leashes. A nylon leash is probably the best option as your Boxer puppy's first leash.

cannot wriggle out of it, but is loose enough so that it will not be uncomfortably tight. You should be able to fit a finger in between the pup's neck and the collar. It may take some time for your pup to get used to wearing the collar, but soon he will not even notice that it is there. Choke collars are made for training, but should only be used by an owner who knows exactly how to use it. If you use a stronger leather leash or a chain leash to walk your Boxer, you will need a stronger collar as well.

FOOD AND WATER BOWLS

Your pup will need two bowls, one for food and one for water. You may want two sets of bowls, one for inside and one for outside, depending on where the dog will be fed and where he will be spending time. Stainless steel or sturdy plastic bowls are popular choices. Although plastic bowls are more chewable, dogs tend not to chew on the steel variety, which can be sterilized. Boxer owners should put their dogs' food and water bowls on specially made elevated stands; this brings the food closer to the dog's level so he does not have to bend down as far, thus aiding his digestion and helping to guard against bloat or gastric torsion in deep-chested dogs. The most important thing is to buy sturdy bowls since, again, anything is in danger of being chewed by puppy teeth and you do not want your dog to be

Your Boxer puppy should be introduced to the collar and leash as soon as possible. It may take a few days for your puppy to become accustomed to a collar.

You will need bowls for food and water. Most breeders opt for stainless steel bowls since they are the most convenient.

PHOTO COURTESY OF MIKKI PET PRODUCTS.

constantly chewing apart his bowl (for his safety and for your wallet).

CLEANING SUPPLIES

Cleaning up messes will be a way of life until your Boxer pup is housebroken. Accidents will occur, which is okay for now because the puppy does not know any better. All you can do is clean up any accidents—old rags, paper towels, newspapers and a safe disinfectant are good to have on hand.

BEYOND THE BASICS

The items previously discussed are the bare necessities. You will find out what else you need as you go along—grooming supplies, flea/tick protection, baby gates to partition a room, etc.—these things will vary depending on your situation. It is just important that right away you have every-thing you need to feed and make your Boxer comfortable in his first few days at home.

PUPPY-PROOFING YOUR HOME

Aside from making sure that your Boxer will be comfortable in your home, you also have to make sure that your home is safe for your Boxer. This means taking precau-tions to make sure that your pup will not get into anything he should not get into and that there is nothing within his reach that may harm him should he sniff it, chew it, inspect it, etc. This probably seems obvious since, while you are primarily concerned with your pup's safety, at the same time you do not want your belongings to be ruined. Breakables should be placed out of reach if your dog is to have full run of the house. If he is to be limited to certain places within the house, keep any potentially dangerous items in the "off-limits" areas. An electrical cord can pose a danger should the puppy decide to taste it—and who is going to convince a pup that it would not make a great chew toy? Cords should be fastened tightly against the wall. If your dog is going to spend time in a crate, make sure that there is nothing near his crate that he can reach if he sticks his curious little nose or paws through the openings. And just as you would with a child, keep all household cleaners and

You will need something to assist you in cleaning up after your Boxer has relieved himself. Pet shops usually have several gadgets suitable for sanitary collection and disposal of waste.

chemicals where the pup cannot get to them.

It is just as important to make sure that the outside of your home is safe. Of course your puppy should never be unsupervised, but a pup let loose in the yard will want to run and explore, and he should be granted that freedom. Do not let a fence give you a false sense of security; you would be surprised how crafty (and persistent) a dog can be in figuring out how to dig under and squeeze his way through small holes, or to jump or climb over a fence. The remedy is to make the fence high enough so that it really is impossible for your dog to get over it (about 6 feet should suffice), and well embedded into the ground. Be sure to repair or secure any gaps or weak spots in the fence. Check the fence periodically to ensure that it is in good shape and

THE CLEAN LIFE

By providing sleeping and resting quarters that fit the dog, and offering him frequent opportunities to relieve himself outside his quarters, the puppy quickly learns that the outdoors is the place to go when he needs to urinate or defecate. It also reinforces his innate desire to keep his sleeping quarters clean. This, in turn, helps develop the muscle control that will eventually produce a dog with clean living habits.

Breakdown of Veterinary Income by Category

2%	Dentistry
4%	Radiology
12%	Surgery
15%	Vaccinations
19%	Laboratory
23%	Examinations
25%	Medicines

make repairs as needed; a very determined pup may return to the same spot to "work on it" until he is able to get through.

FIRST TRIP TO THE VET
Okay, you have picked out your puppy, your home and family are ready, now all you have to do is pick your Boxer up from the breeder and the fun begins, right? Well…not so fast. Something else you need to prepare for is your pup's first trip to the veterinarian. Perhaps the breeder can recommend someone in the area who

specializes in Boxers, or maybe you know some other Boxer owners who can suggest a good vet. Either way, you should have an appointment arranged for your pup before you pick him up; plan on taking him for a checkup within the first few days of bringing him home.

The pup's first visit will consist of an overall examination to make sure that the pup does not have any problems that are not apparent to you. The veterinarian will also set up a schedule for the pup's vaccinations; the breeder will inform you of which ones the pup has already received and the vet can continue from there.

INTRODUCTION TO THE FAMILY
Everyone in the house will be excited about the puppy's coming home and will want to pet him and play with him, but it is best to make the introduction low-key so as not to overwhelm the puppy. He is apprehensive already; it is the first time he has been separated from his mother and the breeder, and the ride to your home is likely the first time he has been in a car. The last thing you want to do is smother him, as this will only frighten him further. This is not to say that human contact is not extremely necessary at this stage, because this is the time when an instant connection

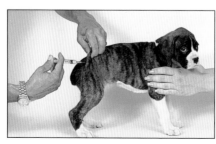

Every Boxer puppy should be vaccinated against a variety of maladies. Follow the advice and direction of your vet. Be punctual and observant of the recommended time schedules.

Boxers have very individual personalities. This fellow likes to collect sticks. Take advantage of these natural instincts and train the dog to bring you the newspaper or your slippers.

between the pup and his human family are formed. Gentle petting and soothing words should help console him, as well as just putting him down and letting him explore on his own (under your watchful eye, of course).

The pup may approach the family members or may busy himself with exploring for a while. Gradually, each person should spend some time with the pup, one at a time, crouching down to get as close to the pup's level as possible and letting him sniff their hands and petting him gently. He definitely needs human attention and he needs to be touched—this is how to form an immediate bond. Just remember that the pup is experiencing a lot of things for the first time, all at the same time. There are new

people, new noises, new smells, and new things to investigate, so be gentle, be affectionate and be as comforting as you can be.

YOUR PUP'S FIRST NIGHT HOME

You have traveled home with your new charge safely in his crate or on a family members lap. He's been to the vet for a thorough check-up; he's been weighed, his papers examined; perhaps he's even been vaccinated and wormed as well. He's met the family and licked the whole family, including the excited children and the less-than-happy cat. He's explored his area, his new bed, the yard and anywhere else he's been permitted. He's eaten his first meal at home and relieved himself in the proper place. He's heard lots of

Meeting a family of potential owners, these Boxer pups are enjoying a picnic in their honor.

Meeting a family of potential owners, these Boxer pups are enjoying a picnic in their honor.

new sounds, smelled new friends and seen more of the outside world than ever before.

That was just the first day! He's exhausted and is ready for bed...or so you think!

It's puppy's first night and you are ready to say "Good night"— keep in mind that this is puppy's first night ever to be sleeping alone. His dam and littermates are no longer at paw's length and he's a bit scared, cold and lonely. Be reassuring to your new family member, but this is not the time to spoil him and give in to his inevitable whining.

Puppies whine. They whine to let the others know where they are and hopefully to get company out of it. Place your pup in his new bed or crate in his room and close the door. Mercifully, he will fall asleep without a peep. When

DEWORMING

Ridding your puppy of worms is very important because they remove the nutrients that a growing puppy needs and certain worms that puppies carry, such as tapeworms and roundworms, can also infect humans.

Breeders initiate deworming programs at or about four weeks of age. The routine is repeated every two or three weeks until the puppy is three months old. The breeder from whom you obtained your puppy should provide you with the complete details of the deworming program.

Your veterinarian can prescribe and monitor the rest of the deworming program for you. The usual program is treating the puppy every 15–20 days until the puppy is positively worm-free. It is advised that you only treat your puppy with drugs that are recommended professionally.

the inevitable occurs, ignore the whining; he is fine. Be strong and keep his interest in mind. Do not allow your heart to become guilty and visit the pup. He will fall asleep.

Many breeders recommend placing a piece of bedding from his former homestead in his new bed so that he recognizes the scent of his littermates. Others still advise placing a hot water bottle in his bed for warmth. This latter may be a good idea, provided the pup doesn't attempt to suckle—he'll get good and wet and may not fall asleep so fast.

Puppy's first night can be somewhat stressful for the pup and his new family. Remember that you are setting the tone of nighttime at your house. Unless you want to play with your pup every night at 10 p.m., midnight and 2 a.m., don't initiate the habit. Surely your family will thank you, and so will your pup!

PREVENTING PUPPY PROBLEMS

SOCIALIZATION

Now that you have done all of the preparatory work and have helped your pup get accustomed to his new home and family, it is about time for you to have some fun! Socializing your Boxer pup gives you the opportunity to show off your new friend, and your pup gets to reap the benefits of being an adorable velvety creature that people will coo over, want to pet and, in general, think is absolutely precious!

Besides getting to know his new family, your puppy should be exposed to other people, animals and situations. This will help him become well adjusted as he grows up and less prone to being timid or fearful of the new things he will encounter. Your pup's socialization began at the breeder's, now it is your responsibility to continue it. The socialization he receives up until the age of 12 weeks is the most critical, as this is the time when he forms his impressions of the outside world. Lack of socialization can manifest itself in fear and aggression as the dog grows up. Your pup needs lots of human contact, affection, handling and exposure to other animals. Be careful during the eight-to-ten-week-old period, also known as the fear period. The interaction he receives from you

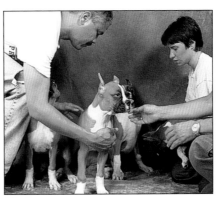

There is no better entertainment for a Boxer puppy of any age than to play with his human friends.

Keep your eye on your Boxer puppy when he is released in the yard. A koi pond is lovely, but it can be dangerous if a puppy decides to chase a fish!

during this time should be gentle and reassuring.

Once your pup has received his necessary vaccinations, feel free to take him out and about (on his leash, of course). Take him around the neighborhood, take him on your daily errands, let people pet him, let him meet other dogs and pets, etc. Puppies do not have to try to make friends; there will be no shortage of people who will want to introduce themselves. Just make sure that you carefully supervise each meeting. If the neighborhood children want to say hello, for example, that is great—children and pups most often make great companions. But sometimes an

excited child can unintentionally handle a pup too roughly, or an overzealous pup can playfully nip a little too hard. You want to make socialization experiences positive ones; what a pup learns during this very formative stage will impact his attitude toward future encounters. A pup that has a bad experience with a child may grow up to be a dog that is shy

EATING IN PEACE
Give your pup his own little corner of the kitchen where he can eat undisturbed and where he will not be underfoot. None of the family members should disturb the pup during his mealtimes.

around or aggressive toward children, and you want your dog to be comfortable around everyone.

CONSISTENCY IN TRAINING

Dogs, being pack animals, naturally need a leader, or else they try to establish dominance in their packs. When you bring a dog into your family, who becomes the leader and who becomes the "pack" are entirely up to you! Your pup's intuitive quest for dominance, coupled with the fact that it is nearly impossible to look at an adorable Boxer pup, with his "puppy-dog" eyes and his lovable expression, and not cave in, give the pup almost an unfair advantage in getting the upper hand! And a pup will definitely test the

PUP MEETS WORLD

Thorough socialization includes not only meeting new people and other pets but also being introduced to new experiences such as riding in the car, having his coat brushed, hearing the television, walking in a crowd—the list is endless. The more your pup experiences, and the more positive the experiences are, the less of a shock and the less frightening it will be for your pup to encounter new things.

waters to see what he can and cannot get away with. Do not give in to those pleading eyes—stand your ground when it comes to disciplining the pup and make sure that all family members do the same. It will only confuse the pup when Mother tells him to get off the couch when he is used to sitting up there with Father to watch the nightly news. Avoid discrepancies by having all members of the household decide on the rules before the pup even comes home...and be consistent

Children's toys are usually unsuitable for Boxer puppies because they are easily shredded, may contain toxic dyes or stuffing or may have wire frames that could injure the dog.

The Boxer puppy's face clearly reveals his dependence and needs. A puppy should never have to wonder if his owner loves him.

in enforcing them! Early training shapes the dog's personality, so you cannot be unclear in what you expect.

COMMON PUPPY PROBLEMS

The best way to prevent problems is to be proactive in stopping an undesirable behavior as soon as it starts. The old saying "You can't teach an old dog new tricks" does not necessarily hold true, but it *is* true that it is much easier to discourage bad behavior in a young developing pup than to wait until the pup's bad behavior becomes the adult dog's bad habit. There are some problems that are especially prevalent in puppies as they develop.

There is no better way for children and puppies to get acquainted than to meet and to exchange smiles and embraces.

NIPPING

As puppies start to teethe, they feel the need to sink their teeth into anything…unfortunately that includes your fingers, arms, hair, toes…whatever happens to be available. You may find this behavior cute for about the first five seconds …until you feel just how sharp those puppy teeth are. This is something you want to discourage immediately and consistently with a firm "No!" (or whatever number of firm "Nos" it takes for him to understand that you mean business) and replace your finger with an appropriate chew toy. While this behavior is merely annoying when the dog is still young, it can become dangerous as your Boxer's adult teeth grow in and his jaws develop, if he thinks that it is okay to gnaw on human appendages. You do not want to take a chance with a Boxer, as this is a breed whose jaws become very strong. He does not mean any harm with a friendly nip, but he also does not know his own strength.

CRYING/WHINING

Your pup will often cry, whine, whimper, howl or make some type of commotion when he is left alone. This is basically his way of calling out for attention, of calling out to make sure that you know he is there and that you have not forgotten about him. He feels insecure when he is left alone, for example, when you are out of the house and he is in his crate or when you are in another part of the house and he cannot see you. The noise he is making is an expression of the anxiety he feels at being alone, so he needs to be taught that being alone is okay. You are not actually training the dog to stop making noise, you are training him to feel comfortable when he is alone and thus removing the need for him to make the noise. This is where the crate with cozy padding and a favorite toy comes in handy. You want to know that he is safe when you are not there to supervise, and you know that he will be safe in his crate rather than roaming freely about the house. In order for the pup to stay in his crate without making a fuss, he needs to be comfortable in his crate. On that note, it is extremely important that the crate is never used as a form of punishment, or the pup will have a negative association with the crate.

Accustom the pup to the crate in short, gradually increasing time

TEMPERAMENT COUNTS

Your selection of a good puppy can be determined by your intentions. A show potential or a good pet? It is your choice. Every puppy, however, should be of good temperament. Although show-quality puppies are bred and raised with emphasis on physical conformation, responsible breeders strive for equally good temperament. Do not buy from a breeder who concentrates solely on physical beauty at the expense of personality.

"Come play with me!" All puppies need playmates to share in a game of ball.

intervals in which you put him in the crate, maybe with a treat, and stay in the room with him. If he cries or makes a fuss, do not go to him, but stay in his sight. Gradually he will realize that staying in his crate is okay without your help, and it will not be so traumatic for him when you are not around. You may want to leave the radio on softly when you leave the house; the sound of human voices may be comforting to him.

Crate-trained adult dogs can be given a "time-out" for some relaxation, such as these Boxers at a dog show.

TAKE HIM TO A TRAINER

Young dogs with mellow personalities and temperaments are much easier to train than more assertive dogs. If you have a puppy that seems untrainable, take him to a trainer or behaviorist. The dog may have a personality problem that requires the help of a professional, or perhaps you need help in learning how to train your dog.

Boxer puppies may look well posed among flowering plants, but take care. Many plants are poisonous to dogs.

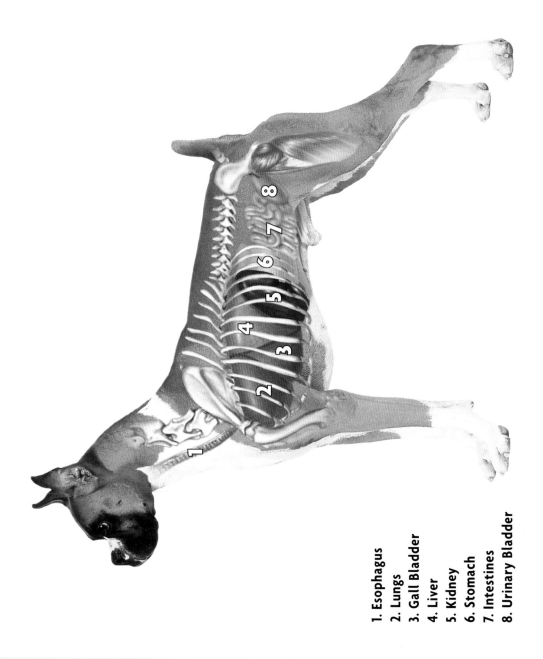

1. Esophagus
2. Lungs
3. Gall Bladder
4. Liver
5. Kidney
6. Stomach
7. Intestines
8. Urinary Bladder

INTERNAL ORGANS OF THE BOXER

Everyday Care of Your Boxer

DIETARY AND FEEDING CONSIDERATIONS

In today's world, the Boxer owner has hundreds of choices for feeding his dog. The market offers dozens of brands in many varieties: from the puppy diet to the lamb and rice to the senior diet to the hypoallergenic to the low-calorie! Since your Boxer's diet is related to his coat, health and temperament, you want to offer him the best possible diet, fit for a Boxer of his age. Owners, however, can become very perplexed by the vast number of choices. Even those people who truly want to feed their dogs the best often cannot do so because they do not know which foods are best for their dogs.

Dog foods are produced in three basic types: dry, semi-moist and canned. Dry foods are for the cost-conscious because they are much less expensive than semi-moist and canned. Dry foods contain the least fat and the most preservatives. Most canned foods are 60–70% water, while semi-moist foods are so full of sugar that they are the least preferred by owners, though dogs welcome them (as does a child candy).

Three stages of development must be considered when selecting a diet for your dog: the puppy stage, the adult stage and the senior stage.

PUPPY DIETS

Puppies have a natural instinct to suck milk from their mother's breasts. They should exhibit this behavior the first day of their

Elevated bowl stands are excellent choices for Boxer adults—and they keep the toddlers away from mom's dish.

Puppies begin
weaning by around
the fourth week,
when the breeder
begins to offer
canned meat.

Puppies begin weaning by around the fourth week, when the breeder begins to offer canned meat.

weeks of their lives. Fortunately, there are good alternatives on the market today.

Puppies should be allowed to nurse for six weeks and they should be slowly weaned away from their mother by introducing small portions of canned meat after they are about one month old. By the time they are eight weeks old, they should be completely weaned and fed solely a suitable puppy food. During the weaning period, selecting their diet is most important as the puppy grows fastest during its first year of life. Growth foods can be recommended by your vet and the puppy should be kept on this diet for up to 18 months. Puppy diets should be balanced for your dog's needs and supplements of vitamins, minerals and protein should not be necessary.

lives. If they don't suckle within an hour, the breeder attempts to put them onto their mother's nipples. Their failure to feed means the breeder has to feed them himself under the guidance of a veterinarian. This involves a baby bottle and a special formula. Their mother's milk is much better than any formula because it contains colostrum, a sort of antibiotic milk, which protects the puppy during the first eight to ten

ADULT DIETS

A dog is considered an adult when he has stopped growing. The growth is in height and/or length. Do not consider the dog's weight when the decision is made to switch from a puppy diet to a maintenance diet. Again you should rely upon your veterinarian to recommend an acceptable maintenance diet. Major dog-food manufacturers specialize in this type of food and it is just necessary for you to select the one best suited to your dog's needs. Active dogs may have different require-

A mother's milk offers puppies the best start in life.

GRAIN-BASED DIETS

Some less expensive dog foods are based on grains and other plant proteins. While these products may appear to be attractively priced, many breeders prefer a diet based on animal proteins and believe that they are more conducive to your dog's health. Many grain-based diets rely on soy protein, which may cause flatulence (passing gas).

There are many cases, however, when your dog might require a special diet. These special requirements should only be recommended by your veterinarian.

ments than sedate dogs. A Boxer reaches adulthood at about two years of age, though some dogs fully mature at 16 months, while others may take up to three years.

SENIOR DIETS

As a dog gets older, his metabolism changes. The older dog usually exercises less, moves more slowly and sleeps more. This change in lifestyle and physiological performance requires a change in diet. Since these changes take place slowly, they might not be recognizable. What is easily recognizable is weight gain. By continually feeding your dog an adult-maintenance diet when it is slowing down metabolically, your dog will gain weight. Obesity in an older dog com-

As your the Boxer matures, his diet should be changed. Consult your vet for advice about when to change the diet and the food you should offer.

The age at which your Boxer reaches full maturity varies depending on the bloodline from which the dog comes and individual bodily development.

pounds the health problems that already accompany old age.

As your dog gets older, few of his organs function up to par. The kidneys slow down and the intestines become less efficient. These age-related factors are best handled with a change in diet and a change in feeding schedule to give smaller portions that are more easily digested.

There is no single best diet for every older dog. While many dogs do well on light or senior diets, other dogs do better on puppy diets or other special premium diets such as lamb and rice. Be sensitive to your senior Boxer's diet and this will help control other problems that may arise with your old friend.

WATER

Just as your dog needs proper nutrition from his food, water is an essential "nutrient" as well. Water keeps the dog's body properly hydrated and promotes normal function of the body's systems. During housebreaking, it is necessary to keep an eye on how much water your Boxer is drinking, but once he is reliably trained he should have access to clean fresh water at all times. Make sure that the dog's water bowl is clean, and change the water often. As some vets have recommended, do not leave water bowls down when feeding your dog. This can help to prevent the onset of bloat in the Boxer.

EXERCISE

Exercising a Boxer is not as daunting as it may seem. The Boxer is a working dog, not a field dog that has pent-up energy or a track dog that has long legs to stretch. All dogs require some form of exercise, regardless of breed. A sedentary lifestyle is as harmful to a dog as it is to a person. The Boxer happens to be a fairly active breed that requires more exercise than, say, an English Bulldog, but you don't have to be a weightlifter or marathon runner to provide your dog with the exercise he needs. Regular walks, play sessions in the yard or letting the dog run free in an enclosed area under your supervision are all sufficient forms of exercise for the Boxer.

The Boxer is a medium-large dog that requires regular exercise periods to keep him physically and mentally fit.

For those who are more ambitious, you will find that your Boxer will be able to keep up with you on extra-long walks or the morning run. Not only is exercise essential to keep the dog's body fit, it is essential to his mental well-being. A bored dog will find something to do, which often manifests itself in some type of destructive behavior. In this sense, it is essential for the owner's mental well-being as well!

Smooth-coated dogs like the Boxer do not require as much grooming as long- or wire-haired breeds, but regular brushing is healthy for the skin and coat nonetheless.

GROOMING YOUR BOXER

BRUSHING

A natural bristle brush, a slicker brush or even a hound glove can be used for regular routine brushing. Grooming is effective for removing dead hair and stimulating the dog's natural oils to add shine and a healthy look to the coat. Your Boxer is not a dog that needs excessive grooming, but his coat needs to be brushed every few days as part of routine maintenance. Regular brushing will get rid of dust and dandruff and remove any dead hair. Regular grooming sessions are also a good way to spend time with your dog. Many dogs grow to like the feel of being brushed and will enjoy the regular routine.

BATHING

Dogs do not need to be bathed as often as humans, but regular bathing is essential for healthy skin and a healthy, shiny coat. Again, like most anything, if you accustom your pup to being bathed as a puppy, it will be second nature by the time he grows up. You want your dog to be at ease in the bath or else it could end up a wet, soapy, messy ordeal for both of you!

Brush your Boxer thoroughly before wetting his coat. This will get rid of most of the dead coat. Make sure that your dog has a good non-slip surface to stand on.

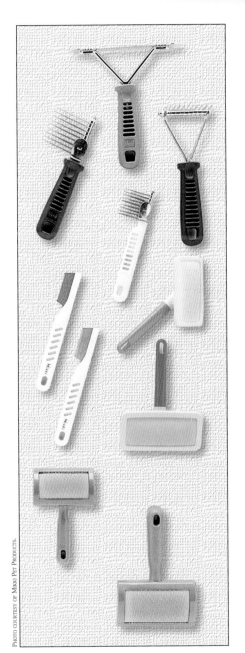

Begin by wetting the dog's coat. A shower or hose attachment is necessary for thoroughly wetting and rinsing the coat. Check the water temperature to make sure that it is neither too hot nor too cold for the dog.

Next, apply shampoo to the dog's coat and work it into a good lather. You should purchase a shampoo that is made for dogs; do not use a product made for human hair. Wash the head last; you do not want shampoo to drip into the dog's eyes while you are washing

Brushing removes dead hair from your Boxer's coat.

Your pet shop sells various grooming tools that are efficient on smooth-coated dogs.

Your local pet shop usually carries a complete range of grooming tools at reasonable prices.

PHOTO COURTESY OF MIKKI PET PRODUCTS.

Most Boxers enjoy water and being bathed. When the temperature permits, you can bathe your Boxer outdoors. If using a water hose for rinsing, do not direct the stream of water at the dog's face, ears or genital area.

Clean your Boxer's ears regularly. Be on the alert for any sign of infection, inflammation or ear mite infestation. Never use a cotton swab in your Boxer's ear.

SOAP IT UP

The use of human soap products like shampoo, bubble bath and hand soap can be damaging to a dog's coat and skin. Human products are too strong; they remove the protective oils coating the dog's hair and skin that make him water-resistant. Use only shampoo made especially for dogs. You may like to use a medicated shampoo, which will help to keep external parasites at bay.

There are "dry bath" products on the market, which are sprays and powders intended for spot cleaning, that can be used between regular baths if necessary. They are not substitutes for regular baths, but they are easy to use for touch-ups as they do not require rinsing.

the rest of his body. Work the shampoo all the way down to the skin. You can use this opportunity to check the skin for any bumps, bites or other abnormalities. Do not neglect any area of the body— get all of the hard-to-reach places.

Once the dog has been thoroughly shampooed, he requires an equally thorough rinsing. Shampoo left in the coat can be irritating to the skin. Protect his eyes from the shampoo by shielding them with your hand and directing the flow of water in the opposite direction. You should also avoid getting water in the ear canal. Be prepared for your dog to

Your Boxer's nails will require clipping through-out his life. You should learn how to clip your Boxer's nails and accustom your dog to the routine while he is still a puppy.

GROOMING EQUIPMENT

How much grooming equipment you purchase will depend on how much grooming you are going to do. Here are some basics:
- Natural bristle brush
- Slicker brush
- Grooming glove
- Scissors
- Rubber mat
- Dog shampoo
- Spray hose attachment
- Heavy towels
- Ear cleaner
- Cotton balls
- Nail clippers

shake out his coat—you might want to stand back, but make sure you have a hold on the dog to keep him from running through the house.

EAR CLEANING

The ears should be kept clean and any excess hair inside the ear should be trimmed. Ears can be cleaned with a cotton ball and special cleaner or ear powder made for dogs. Be on the lookout for any signs of infection or ear-mite infestation. If your Boxer has been shaking his head or scratch-ing at his ears frequently, this usually indicates a problem. If his

PEDICURE TIP

A dog that spends a lot of time outside on a hard surface, such as cement or pavement, will have his nails naturally worn down and may not need to have them trimmed as often, except maybe in the colder months when he is not outside as much. Regardless, it is best to get your dog accustomed to the nail-trimming procedure at an early age so that he is used to it. Some dogs are especially sensitive about having their feet touched, but if a dog has experienced it since puppyhood, it should not bother him. A nail grinder is an excellent alternative for Boxers that are sensitive about their feet.

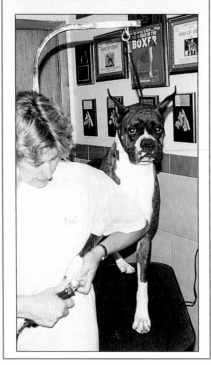

ears have an unusual odor, this is a sure sign of mite infestation or infection, and a signal to have his ears checked by the vet.

NAIL CLIPPING

Your Boxer should be accustomed to having his nails trimmed at an early age, since it will be part of your maintenance routine throughout his life. Not only does it look nicer, but a dog with long nails can cause injury if he jumps up and scratches someone unintentionally. Also, a long nail has a better chance of ripping and bleeding, or causing the feet to spread. A good rule of thumb is that if you can hear your dog's

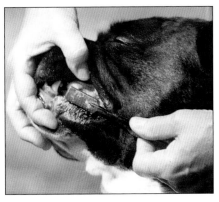

hand, simply take off the end of each nail in one quick clip. You can purchase nail clippers that are specially made for dogs; you can probably find them wherever you buy grooming supplies.

nails' clicking on the floor when he walks, his nails are too long.

Before you start cutting, make sure you can identify the "quick" in each nail. The quick is a blood vessel that runs through the center of each nail and grows rather close to the end. It will bleed if accidentally cut, which will be quite painful for the dog as it contains nerve endings. Keep some type of clotting agent on hand, such as a styptic pencil or styptic powder (the type used for shaving). This will stop the bleeding quickly when applied to the end of the cut nail. Do not panic if this happens, just stop the bleeding and talk soothingly to your dog. Once he has calmed down, move on to the next nail. It is better to clip a little at a time, particularly with black-nailed dogs.

Hold your pup steady as you begin trimming his nails; you do not want him to make any sudden movements or run away. Talk to him soothingly and stroke him as you clip. Holding his foot in your

There are scissors with rounded tips to trim facial hairs and whiskers from your Boxer's face, if so desired.

Immaculate grooming requires trimming excess hair growth wherever it occurs.

Caring for your Boxer's teeth requires regular brushing and use of dental chew devices available from your pet shop. Use special toothbrushes designed specifically for dogs.

TRAVELING WITH YOUR DOG

CAR TRAVEL

You should accustom your Boxer to riding in a car at an early age. You may or may not often take him in the car, but at the very least he will need to go to the vet and you do not want these trips to be traumatic for the dog or a big hassle for you. The safest way for a dog to ride in the car is in his crate. If he uses a fiberglass crate in the house, you can use the same crate for travel. If you have a wire crate in the house, consider purchasing an appropriately sized fiberglass or wooden crate for traveling. Wire crates can be used for travel, but fiberglass or wooden crates are sturdier.

Put the pup in the crate and see how he reacts. If he seems uneasy, you can have a passenger hold him on his lap while you drive. Another option is a specially made safety harness for dogs, which straps the dog in

There are special crates in which your Boxer can be safely transported in your vehicle. Never allow the dog to go unrestrained while you are driving.

> **TRAVEL TIP**
> Never leave your dog alone in the car. In hot weather, your dog can die from the high temperature inside a closed vehicle; even a car parked in the shade can heat up very quickly. Leaving the window open is dangerous as well since the dog can hurt himself trying to get out.

much like a seat belt. Do not let the dog roam loose in the vehicle—this is very dangerous! If you should stop short, your dog can be thrown and injured. If the dog starts climbing on you and pestering you while you are driving, you will not be able to concentrate on the road. It is an unsafe situation for everyone—human and canine.

For long trips, be prepared to stop to let the dog relieve himself. Bring along whatever you need to clean up after him. You should bring along some paper towels and rags, should he have an accident in the car or become carsick.

AIR TRAVEL

If bringing your dog on a flight, you will have to contact the airline to make special arrangements. It is rather common for dogs to travel by air, but advance permission is always required. The dog will be required to travel in a fiberglass crate; you may be able to use your own or the airline may supply one. To help the dog be at ease, put one of his favorite toys in the crate with him. Do not feed the dog for several hours before the trip to minimize his need to relieve himself. You may need to provide documentation as to when the dog has last been fed; in any case, a light meal is best.

Make sure your dog is properly identified and that your contact information appears on his ID tags and on his crate. Animals travel in a different area of the plane than human passengers, and, although transporting animals is routine for large airlines, there is always a slight risk of getting separated from your dog.

Special restraining halters can be used on many occasions. Your Boxer can be outfitted with a halter to use like a seat belt in the car, for example.

VACATIONS AND BOARDING

So you want to take a family vacation—and you want to include *all* members of the family. You would probably make arrangements for accommodations ahead of time anyway, but this is especially important when traveling with a dog. You do not want to make an overnight stop at the only place

TRAVELING ABROAD

For international travel, you will have to make arrangements well in advance (perhaps months), as countries' regulations pertaining to bringing in animals differ. There may be special health certificates and/or vaccinations that your dog will need before taking the trip; sometimes this has to be done within a certain time frame. In rabies-free countries, you will need to bring proof of the dog's rabies vaccination and there may be a quarantine period upon arrival.

Boxer owners should have ample vehicle space to travel with their dogs.

around for miles to find out that they do not allow dogs. Also, you do not want to reserve a place for your family without mentioning that you are bringing a dog, because if it is against their policy you may not have a place to stay.

Alternatively, if you are traveling and choose not to bring your Boxer, you will have to make arrangements for him while you are away. Some options are to bring him to a neighbor's house to stay while you are gone, to have a trusted neighbor stop by often or stay at your house or to bring your dog to a reputable boarding kennel. If you choose to board

COLLAR REQUIRED
If your dog gets lost, he is not able to ask for directions home. Identification tags fastened to the collar give important information—the dog's name, the owner's name, the owner's address and a telephone number where the owner can be reached. This makes it easy for whomever finds the dog to contact the owner and arrange to have the dog returned. An added advantage is that a person will be more likely to approach a lost dog who has ID tags on his collar; it tells the person that this is somebody's pet rather than a stray. This is the easiest and fastest method of identification, provided that the tags stay on the collar and the collar stays on the dog.

Bonding is required between dogs as well as between people. Unless dogs know each other, they should be supervised, especially when one is much smaller than the other.

him at a kennel, you should stop by to see the facility and where the dogs are kept to make sure that it is clean. Talk to some of the employees and see how they treat the dogs—do they spend time with the dogs, play with them, exercise them, etc.? You know that your Boxer will not be happy unless he gets regular activity. Also find out the kennel's policy on vaccinations and what they require. This is for all of the dogs' safety, since when dogs are kept together, there is a greater risk of diseases being passed from dog to dog. Many veterinarians offer boarding facilities; this is another option.

IDENTIFICATION

Your Boxer is your valued companion and friend. That is why you always keep a close eye on him and you have made sure that he cannot escape from the yard or wriggle out of his collar and run away from you. However, accidents can happen and there may come a time when your dog unexpectedly gets separated from you. If this unfortunate event should occur, the first thing on your mind will be finding him. Proper identification will increase the chances of his being returned to you safely and quickly.

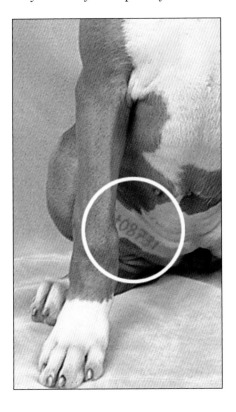

IDENTIFICATION OPTIONS

As puppies become more and more expensive, especially those puppies of high quality for showing and/or breeding, they have a greater chance of being stolen. The usual collar dog tag is, of course, easily removed. But there are two more permanent techniques that have become widely used for identification.

The puppy microchip implantation involves the injection of a small microchip, about the size of a corn kernel, under the skin of the dog. If your dog shows up at a clinic or shelter, or is offered for resale under less-than-savory circumstances, he can be positively identified by the microchip. The microchip is scanned, and a registry quickly identifies you as the owner.

Tattooing is done on various parts of the dog, from his belly to his ears. The number tattooed can be your telephone number or any other number that you can easily memorize. When professional dog thieves see a tattooed dog, they usually lose interest. For the safety of our dogs, no laboratory facility or dog broker will accept a tattooed dog as stock.

Discuss microchipping and tattooing with your veterinarian and breeder. Some vets perform these services on their own premises for a reasonable fee. In order to ensure the effectiveness of your Boxer's identification, be certain that the dog is then properly registered with a legitimate national database.

Tattoos are recommended for identifying your dog. The tattoo is often located inside the rear thigh. In short-coated breeds like the Boxer, tattoos are easily visible in this area.

A Boxer must be trained. An undisciplined Boxer is simply not enjoyable as a house pet. The more effort you put into training, the more you will enjoy your dog. Invest time when he is still young and you will reap the benefits for the life of the dog.

Training Your Boxer

Living with an untrained dog is a lot like owning a piano that you do not know how to play—it is a nice object to look at, but it does not do much more than that to bring you pleasure. Now try taking piano lessons, and suddenly the piano comes alive and brings forth magical sounds and rhythms that set your heart singing and your body swaying.

The same is true with your Boxer. At first you enjoy seeing him around the house. He does not do much with you other than to need food, water and exercise. Come to think of it, he does not bring you much joy, either. He is a big responsibility with a very small return. And often, he develops unacceptable behaviors that annoy you, to say nothing of bad habits that may end up costing you great sums of money. Not a good thing!

Now train your Boxer. Enroll in an obedience class. Teach him good manners as you learn how and why he behaves the way he does. Find out how to communicate with your dog and how to recognize and understand his communications with you.

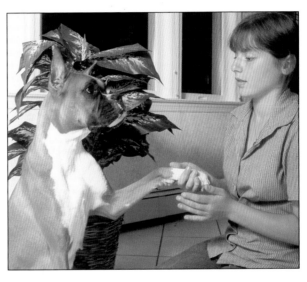

Suddenly the dog takes on a new role in your life—he is smart, interesting, well behaved and fun to be with, and he demonstrates his bond of devotion to you daily. In other words, your Boxer does wonders for your ego because he constantly reminds you that you are not only his leader, you are his hero! Miraculous things have happened—you have a wonderful dog (even your family and friends have noticed the transformation!) and you feel good about yourself.

Those involved with teaching dog obedience and counseling

"Paw" or "Shake" is a common parlor trick that dog owners teach their dogs, though it is not one of the essential commands. It's easy to teach and can be used at the end of each lesson to finish with a positive, successful, fun exercise.

owners about their dogs' behavior have discovered some interesting facts about dog ownership. For example, training dogs when they are puppies results in the highest rate of success in developing well-mannered and well-adjusted adult dogs. Training an older dog, say from six months to six years of age, can produce almost equal results, providing that the owner accepts the dog's slower rate of learning capability and is willing to work patiently to help the dog succeed at developing to his fullest potential. Unfortunately, the patience factor is what many owners of untrained adult dogs lack, so they do not persist until their dogs are successful at learning particular behaviors.

Training a puppy, for example, aged 8 to 16 weeks (20 weeks at the most) is like working with a dry sponge in a pool of water. The pup soaks up whatever you show him and constantly looks for more things to do and learn. At this early age, his body is not yet producing hormones, and therein lies the reason for such a high rate of success. Without hormones, he is focused on his owners and not particularly interested in investigating other places, dogs, people, etc. You are his leader; his provider of food, water, shelter and security. Therefore, he latches onto you and wants to stay close. He will usually follow you from room to room, will not let you out of his sight when you are outdoors with him and will respond in like manner to the people and animals you encounter. If, for example, you greet a friend warmly, he will be happy to greet the person as well. If, however, you are hesitant or anxious about the approach of a stranger, he will respond accordingly to that person.

Once the puppy begins to produce hormones, his natural curiosity emerges and he begins to investigate the world around him. It is at that time when you may notice that the untrained dog begins to wander away from you and even ignore your commands to stay close. When this behavior becomes a problem, the owner has two choices: get rid of the dog or train him. It is strongly urged that you choose the latter option.

Occasionally there are no classes available within a reasonable distance from the owner's home. Sometimes there are classes available but the tuition is too

TRAINING RULES

If you want to be successful in training your dog, you have four rules to obey yourself:

1. Develop an understanding of how a dog thinks.
2. Do not blame the dog for lack of communication.
3. Define your dog's personality and act accordingly.
4. Have patience and be consistent.

Puppies are impressionable and approachable. This Boxer puppy is happily socializing with an affable, long-eared visitor.

costly. Whatever the circumstances, the solution to training your Boxer without formal obedience lessons lies within the pages of this book.

This chapter is devoted to helping you train your Boxer at home. If the recommended procedures are followed faithfully, you may expect positive results that will prove rewarding to both you and your dog.

Whether your Boxer is a puppy or a mature adult, the methods of teaching and the techniques we use in training basic behaviors are the same. After all, no dog, whether puppy or adult, likes harsh or inhumane methods. All creatures, however, respond favorably to gentle motivational methods and sincere praise and encouragement. Now let us get started.

HOUSEBREAKING

You can train a puppy to relieve himself wherever you choose. For example, city dwellers often train their dogs to relieve themselves at the curbside because large plots of grass are not readily available. Suburbanites, on the other hand, usually have yards to accommodate their dogs' needs.

Outdoor training includes such surfaces as grass, dirt and cement. Indoor training usually means training your dog to newspaper. When deciding on the surface and location that you will want your Boxer to use, be sure it is going to be permanent. Training your dog to grass and then changing your mind two months later is extremely difficult for both dog and owner.

sleeping and any time he indicates that he is looking for a place to urinate or defecate. The urinary and intestinal tract muscles of very young puppies are not fully developed. Therefore, like human babies, puppies need to relieve themselves frequently.

Take your puppy out often—every hour for an eight-week-old, for example. The older the puppy, the less often he will need to relieve himself. Finally, as a mature healthy adult, he will require only three to five relief trips per day.

HOUSING

Since the types of housing and control you provide for your puppy have a direct relationship on the success of house-training, we consider the various aspects of both before we begin training.

Next, choose the command you will use each and every time you want your puppy to void. "Go hurry up" and "Go make" are examples of commands commonly used by dog owners. Get in the habit of asking the puppy, "Do you want to go hurry up?" (or whatever your chosen relief command is) before you take him out. That way, when he becomes an adult, you will be able to determine if he wants to go out when you ask him. A confirmation will be signs of interest such as wagging his tail, watching you intently, going to the door, etc.

PUPPY'S NEEDS

The puppy needs to relieve himself after play periods, after each meal, after he has been

> **HOUSE-TRAINING TIP**
>
> Most of all, be consistent. Always take your dog to the same location, always use the same command and always have the dog on lead when he is in his relief area, unless a fenced-in yard is available.
>
> By following the prescribed method, your puppy will be completely housebroken by the time his muscle and brain development reach maturity. Keep in mind that small breeds usually mature faster than large breeds, but all puppies should be trained by six months of age.

Canine Development Schedule

It is important to understand how and at what age a puppy develops into adulthood. If you are a puppy owner, consult the following Canine Development Schedule to determine the stage of development your Boxer puppy is currently experiencing. This knowledge will help you as you work with the puppy in the weeks and months ahead.

Period	Age	Characteristics
First to Third	**Birth to Seven Weeks**	Puppy needs food, sleep and warmth, and responds to simple and gentle touching. Needs mother for security and disciplining. Needs littermates for learning and interacting with other dogs. Pup learns to function within a pack and learns pack order of dominance. Begin socializing with adults and children for short periods. Begins to become aware of his environment.
Fourth	**Eight to Twelve Weeks**	Brain is fully developed. Needs socializing with outside world. Remove from mother and littermates. Needs to change from canine pack to human pack. Human dominance necessary. Fear period occurs between 8 and 16 weeks. Avoid fright and pain.
Fifth	**Thirteen to Sixteen Weeks**	Training and formal obedience should begin. Less association with other dogs, more with people, places, situations. Period will pass easily if you remember this is pup's change-to-adolescence time. Be firm and fair. Flight instinct prominent. Permissiveness and over-disciplining can do permanent damage. Praise for good behavior.
Juvenile	**Four to Eight Months**	Another fear period about 7 to 8 months of age. It passes quickly, but be cautious of fright and pain. Sexual maturity reached. Dominant traits established. Dog should understand sit, down, come and stay by now.

NOTE: THESE ARE APPROXIMATE TIME FRAMES. ALLOW FOR INDIVIDUAL DIFFERENCES IN PUPPIES.

As active as puppies can be, they also need frequent breaks to rest and nap just like young children.

Bringing a new puppy home and turning him loose in your house can be compared to turning a child loose in a sports arena and telling the child that the place is all his! The sheer enormity of the place would be too much for him to handle.

Instead, offer the puppy clearly defined areas where he can play, sleep, eat and live. A room of the house where the family gathers is the most obvious choice. Puppies are social animals and need to feel a part of the pack right from the start. Hearing your voice, watching you while you are doing things and smelling you nearby are all positive reinforcers that he is now a member of your pack. Usually a family room, the kitchen or a nearby adjoining breakfast nook is ideal for providing safety and security for both puppy and owner.

Within that room, there should be a smaller area that the puppy can call his own. A cubby-hole, a wire or fiberglass dog crate or a gated (not boarded!) corner from which he can view the activities of his new family will be fine. The size of the area or crate

is the key factor here. The area must be large enough for the puppy to lie down and stretch out as well as stand up without rubbing his head on the top, yet small enough so that he cannot relieve himself at one end and sleep at the other without coming into contact with his droppings.

Dogs are, by nature, clean animals and will not remain close to their relief areas unless forced to do so. In those cases, they then become dirty dogs and usually remain that way for life.

The crate or cubby should be lined with a clean towel and offer one toy, no more. Do not put food or water in the crate, as eating and drinking will activate his digestive processes and ultimately defeat your purpose as well as make the puppy very uncomfortable as he attempts to "hold it."

CONSISTENCY PAYS OFF

Dogs need consistency in their feeding schedule, exercise and relief visits, and in the verbal commands you use. If you use "Stay" on Monday and "Stay here, please" on Tuesday, you will confuse your dog. Don't demand perfect behavior during training sessions and then let him have the run of the house the rest of the day. Above all, lavish praise on your pet consistently every time he does something right. The more he feels he is pleasing you, the more willing he will be to learn.

CONTROL

By *control*, we mean helping the puppy to create a lifestyle pattern that will be compatible to that of his human pack *(you!)*. Just as we guide little children to learn our way of life, we must show the puppy when it is time to play, eat, sleep, exercise and even entertain himself.

Your puppy should always sleep in his crate. He should also learn that, during times of household confusion and excessive human activity such as at breakfast when family members are preparing for the day, he can play by himself in relative safety and comfort in his crate. Each time you leave the puppy alone, he should be crated. Puppies are chewers. They cannot tell the difference between things like lamp cords, television wires, shoes, table legs, etc. Chewing into a television wire, for example, can be fatal to the puppy, while a shorted wire can start a fire in the house.

If the puppy chews on the chair when he is alone, you will probably discipline him angrily when you get home. Thus, he makes the association that your coming home means he is going to be scolded or punished. (He will not remember chewing the chair and is incapable of making the association of the discipline with his naughty deed.)

Other times of excitement, such as visits, family parties, etc., can be fun for the puppy, providing he can view the activities

"Why doesn't this Boxer get into trouble?" wonders a confused eight-week-old.

PAPER CAPER

Never line your pup's sleeping area with newspaper. Puppy litters are usually raised on newspaper and, once in your home, the puppy will immediately associate newspaper with voiding. Never put newspaper on any floor while house-training, as this will only confuse the puppy. If you are paper-training him, use paper in his designated relief area only. Finally, restrict water after evening meals. Offer a few licks at a time—never let a Boxer of any age gulp water after meals.

SCHEDULE

As stated earlier, a puppy should be taken to his relief area each time he is released from his crate, after meals, after play sessions, when he first awakens in the morning (at age 8 weeks, this can mean 5 a.m.!) and whenever he indicates by circling or sniffing busily that he needs to urinate or defecate. For a puppy less than ten weeks of age, a routine of taking him out every hour is necessary. As the puppy grows, he will be able to wait for longer periods of time.

Keep trips to his relief area short. Stay no more than five or six minutes and then return to the house. If he goes during that time, praise him lavishly and take him indoors immediately. If he does not, but he has an accident when you go back indoors, pick him up immediately, say "No! No!" and return to his relief area. Wait a few minutes, then return to the house again. *Never* hit a puppy or put his face in urine or excrement when he has an accident!

Once indoors, put the puppy in his crate until you have time to clean up his accident. Then release him to the family area and watch him more closely than before. Chances are, his accident was a result of your not picking up his signal or waiting too long before offering him the opportunity to relieve himself. *Never* hold a grudge against the puppy for accidents.

from the security of his crate. He is not underfoot and he is not being fed all sorts of tidbits that will probably cause him stomach distress, yet he still feels a part of the fun.

Let the puppy learn that going outdoors means it is time to relieve himself, not play. Once trained, he will be able to play indoors and out and still differentiate between the times for play versus the times for relief.

Help him develop regular hours for naps, being alone, playing by himself and just resting, all in his crate. Encourage him to entertain himself while you are busy with your activities. Let him learn that having you near is comforting, but it is not your main purpose in life to provide him with undivided attention.

Each time you put your puppy in his crate, tell him "Crate time!" (or whatever command you choose). Soon, he will run to his crate when he hears you say those words.

In the beginning of his training, do not leave him in his crate for prolonged periods of time except during the night when everyone is sleeping. Make his experience with his crate a pleasant one and, as an adult, he will love his crate and willingly stay in it for several hours. There are millions of people who go to work every day and leave their adult dogs crated while they are away. The dogs accept this as their lifestyle and look forward to "crate time."

Crate training provides safety for you, the puppy and the home. It also provides the puppy with a feeling of security, and that helps the puppy achieve self-confidence and clean habits. Remember that one of the primary ingredients in house-training your puppy is control. Regardless of your lifestyle, there will always be occasions when you will need to have a place where your dog can stay and be happy and safe. Crate training is the answer for now and in the future.

In conclusion, a few key elements are really all you need for a successful house- and crate-training method—consistency, frequency, praise, control and supervision. By following these procedures with a normal, healthy puppy, you and the puppy will soon be past the stage of "accidents" and ready to move on to a clean and rewarding life together.

ROLES OF DISCIPLINE, REWARD AND PUNISHMENT

Discipline, training one to act in accordance with rules, brings order to life. It is as simple as

Male Boxers will mark their territory in a most familiar manner.

that. Without discipline, particularly in a group society, chaos reigns supreme and the group will eventually perish. Humans and canines are social animals and need some form of discipline in order to function effectively. They must procure food, reproduce to keep the species going and protect their home base and their young. If there were no discipline in the lives of social animals, they would eventually die from starvation and/or predation by other stronger animals. In the case of domestic canines, dogs need discipline in their lives in order to understand how their pack (you

THE SUCCESS METHOD

Success that comes by luck is usually short-lived. Success that comes by well-thought-out proven methods is often more easily achieved and permanent. This is the Success Method. It is designed to give you, the puppy owner, a simple yet proven way to help your puppy develop clean living habits and a feeling of security in his new environment.

6 Steps to Successful Crate Training

1 Tell the puppy "Crate time!" and place him in the crate with a small treat (a piece of cheese or half of a biscuit). Let him stay in the crate for five minutes while you are in the same room. Then release him and praise lavishly. Never release him when he is fussing. Wait until he is quiet before you let him out.

2 Repeat Step 1 several times a day.

3 The next day, place the puppy in the crate as before. Let him stay there for ten minutes. Do this several times.

4 Continue building time in five-minute increments until the puppy stays in his crate for 30 minutes with you in the room. Always take him to his relief area after prolonged periods in his crate.

5 Now go back to Step 1 and let the puppy stay in his crate for five minutes, this time while you are out of the room.

6 Once again, build crate time in five-minute increments with you out of the room. When the puppy will stay willingly in his crate (he may even fall asleep!) for 30 minutes with you out of the room, he will be ready to stay in it for several hours at a time.

and other family members) functions and how they must act in order to survive.

A large humane society in a highly populated area recently surveyed dog owners regarding their satisfaction with their relationships with their dogs. People who had trained their dogs were 75% more satisfied with their pets than those who had never trained their dogs.

Dr. Edward Thorndike, a noted psychologist, established *Thorndike's Theory of Learning*, which states that a behavior that results in a pleasant event tends to be repeated. Likewise, a behavior that results in an unpleasant event tends not to be repeated. It is this theory on which training methods are based today. For example, if you manipulate a dog to perform a specific behavior and reward him for doing it, he is likely to do it again because he enjoyed the end result.

Occasionally, punishment, a penalty inflicted for an offense, is necessary. The best type of punishment often comes from an outside source. For example, a child is told not to touch the stove because he may get burned. He disobeys and touches the stove. In doing so, he receives a burn. From that time on, he respects the heat of the stove and avoids contact with it. Therefore, a behavior that results in an unpleasant event tends not to be repeated.

A good example of a dog learning the hard way is the dog who chases the house cat. He is told many times to leave the cat alone, yet he persists in teasing the cat. Then, one day he begins chasing the cat but the cat turns and swipes a claw across the dog's face, leaving him with a painful gash on his nose. The final result is that the dog stops chasing the cat.

TRAINING EQUIPMENT

COLLAR
The collar used for training a Boxer must be flexible and light, but strong enough to control the dog. The dog's everyday leather collar is not ideal for training purposes, but a nylon choke collar will give the handler more control of the dog. Do not use a

This is the correct way to use a choke chain.

will forget why he is being rewarded in the first place! Keep in mind that using food rewards will not teach a dog to beg at the table—the only way to teach a dog to beg at the table is to give him food from the table. In training, rewarding the dog with a food treat away from the table will help him associate praise and the treats with learning new behaviors that obviously please his owner.

TRAINING BEGINS: ASK THE DOG A QUESTION

In order to teach your dog anything, you must first get his attention. After all, he cannot learn anything if he is looking away from you with his mind on something else.

To get his attention, ask him "School?" and immediately walk over to him and give him a treat

chain choke collar on the Boxer, as it can damage the dog's hair around the neck. Never leave a choke collar on the dog when not training.

LEASH
A 6-foot leash is recommended, preferably made of leather, nylon or heavy cloth. A chain lead is not recommended, as many dog owners find that these are too heavy for the Boxer.

TREATS
Have a bag of treats on hand. Something nutritious and easy to swallow works best; use a soft treat, a chunk of cheese or a piece of cooked chicken rather than a dry biscuit. By the time the dog gets done chewing a dry treat, he

LANGUAGE BARRIER
Dogs do not understand our language and have to rely on tone of voice more than just words or sound. They can be trained to react to a certain sound, at a certain volume. If you say "No, Oliver" in a very soft, pleasant voice, it will not have the same meaning as "No, Oliver!!" when you raise your voice. You should never use the dog's name during a reprimand, just the command "No! " You never want the dog to associate his name with a negative experience or reprimand.

as you tell him "Good dog." Wait a minute or two and repeat the routine, this time with a treat in your hand as you approach to within a foot of him. Do not go directly to him, but stop about a foot short of him and hold out the treat as you ask "School?" He will see you approaching with a treat in your hand and most likely begin walking toward you. As you meet, give him the treat and praise again.

The third time, ask the question, have a treat in your hand and walk only a short distance toward the dog so that he must walk almost all the way to you. As he reaches you, give him the treat and praise again.

By this time, the dog will probably be getting the idea that if he pays attention to you, especially when you ask that question, it will pay off in treats and fun activities for him. In other words, he learns that "school" means doing fun things with you that result in treats and positive attention for him.

Remember that the dog does not understand your verbal language, he only recognizes sounds. Your question translates to a series of sounds for him, and those sounds become the signal to go to you and pay attention; if he does, he will get to interact with you plus receive treats and praise.

Treats as rewards are effective for use in training the Boxer.

THE BASIC COMMANDS

TEACHING SIT
Now that you have the dog's attention, hold the leash in your left hand and the food treat in

Teaching the Boxer to sit is one of the easiest commands to accomplish. Therefore, it is wise to use the sit command as a starting point.

your right. Place your food hand at the dog's nose and let him lick the treat but not take it from you. Say "Sit" and slowly raise your food hand from in front of the dog's nose up over his head so that he is looking at the ceiling. As he bends his head upward, he will have to bend his knees to maintain his balance. As he bends his knees, he will assume a sit position. At that point, release the food treat and praise lavishly with comments such as "Good dog! Good sit!," etc. Remember to always praise enthusiastically, because dogs relish verbal praise

A little pressure on the hindquarters of a stubborn student may be all that is needed to reinforce the sit command.

> **PRACTICE MAKES PERFECT!**
> - Have training lessons with your dog every day in several short segments—three to five times a day for a few minutes at a time is ideal.
> - Do not have long practice sessions. The dog will become easily bored.
> - Never practice when you are tired, ill, worried or in an otherwise negative mood. This will transmit to the dog and may have an adverse effect on his performance.
>   Think fun, short and above all *positive!* End each session on a high note, rather than a failed exercise, and make sure to give a lot of praise. Enjoy the training and help your dog enjoy it, too.

from their owners and feel so proud of themselves whenever they accomplish a behavior.

You will not use food forever in getting the dog to obey your commands. Food is only used to teach new behaviors and, once the dog knows what you want when you give a specific command, you will wean him off the food treats but still maintain the verbal praise. After all, you should always have your voice with you, but there will be many times when you have no food rewards yet you expect the dog to obey.

TEACHING DOWN
Teaching the down exercise is easy when you understand how the dog perceives the down posi-

tion, and it is very difficult when you do not. In addition, teaching the down exercise using the wrong method can sometimes make the dog develop such a fear of the down that he either runs away when you say "Down" or he attempts to bite the person who tries to force him down.

Have the dog sit close alongside your left leg, facing in the same direction as you are. Hold the leash in your left hand and a food treat in your right. Now place your left hand lightly on the top of the dog's shoulders where they meet above the spinal cord. Do not push down on the dog's shoulders; simply rest your left hand there so you can guide the dog to lie down close to your left leg rather than to swing away from your side when he drops.

Now place the food hand at the dog's nose, say "Down" very softly (almost a whisper) and slowly lower the food hand to the dog's front feet. When the food

Three steps in teaching your dog the down exercise. You must be gentle and reassuring when teaching the down.

DOUBLE JEOPARDY
A dog in jeopardy never lies down. He stays alert on his feet because instinct tells him that he may have to run away or fight for his survival. Therefore, if a dog feels threatened or anxious, he will not lie down. Consequently, it is important to keep the dog calm and relaxed as he learns the down exercise.

Once the Boxer has learned the stay command, you can add distance between you and the dog.

TEACHING STAY

It is easy to teach the dog to stay in either a sit or a down position. Again, we use food and praise during the teaching process as we help the dog to understand exactly what it is that we are expecting him to do.

To teach the sit/stay, start with the dog sitting on your left side as before and hold the leash in your left hand. Have a food treat in your right hand and place your food hand at the dog's nose. Say "Stay" and step out on your right foot to

hand reaches the floor, begin moving it forward along the floor in front of the dog. Keep talking softly to the dog, saying things like, "Do you want this treat? You can do this, good dog." Your reassuring tone of voice will help calm the dog as he tries to follow the food hand in order to get the treat.

When the dog's elbows touch the floor, release the food and praise softly. Try to get the dog to maintain that down position for several seconds before you let him sit up again. The goal here is to get the dog to settle down and not feel threatened in the down position.

Teaching the stay command in the down position.

"COME" . . . BACK

Never call your dog to come to you for a correction or scold him when he reaches you. That is the quickest way to turn a come command into "Go away fast!" Dogs think only in the present tense, and your dog will connect the scolding with coming to you, not with the misbehavior of a few moments earlier.

---

stand directly in front of the dog, toe to toe, as he licks and nibbles the treat. Be sure to keep his head facing upward to maintain the sit position. Count to five and then swing around to stand next to the dog again with him on your left. As soon as you get back to the original position, release the food and praise lavishly.

To teach the down/stay, do the down as previously described. As soon as the dog lies down, say

"Stay" and step out on your right foot just as you did in the sit/stay. Count to five and then return to stand beside the dog with him on your left side. Release the treat and praise as always.

Within a week to ten days, you can begin to add a bit of distance between you and your dog when you leave him. When you do, use your left hand open with the palm facing the dog as a stay signal, much the same as the hand signal a police officer uses to stop traffic at an intersection. Hold the food treat in your right hand as before, but this time the food is not touching the dog's nose. He will watch the food hand and quickly learn that he is going to get that treat as soon as you return to his side.

When you can stand 3 feet away from your dog for 30 seconds, you can then begin building time and distance in both stays. Eventually, the dog can be expected to remain in the stay position for prolonged periods of time until you return to him or call him to you. Always praise lavishly when he stays.

TEACHING COME

If you make teaching "come" a fun experience, you should never have a student that does not love the game or that fails to come when called. The secret, it seems, is never to teach the word "come."

At times when an owner most wants his dog to come when called, the owner is likely upset or anxious and he allows these feelings to come through in the tone of his voice when he calls his dog. Hearing that desperation in his owner's voice, the dog fears the results of going to him and therefore either disobeys outright or runs in the opposite direction. The secret, therefore, is to teach the dog a game and, when you want him to come to you, simply play the game. It is practically a no-fail solution!

To begin, have several members of your family take a few food treats and each go into a

REAP THE REWARDS

If you start with a normal, healthy dog and give him time, patience and some carefully executed lessons, you will reap the rewards of that training for the life of the dog. And what a life it will be! The two of you will find immeasurable pleasure in the companionship you have built together with love, respect and understanding.

different room in the house. Take turns calling the dog, and each person should celebrate the dog's finding him with a treat and lots of happy praise. When a person calls the dog, he is actually inviting the dog to find him and get a treat as a reward for "winning."

A few turns of the "Where are you?" game and the dog will figure out that everyone is playing the game and that each person has a big celebration awaiting the dog's success at locating the person. Once he learns to love the game, simply calling out "Where are you?" will bring him running from wherever he is when he hears that all-important question.

The come command is recognized as one of the most important things to teach a dog, but it is interesting to note that there are trainers who work with thousands of dogs and never teach the actual word "come." Yet these dogs will race to respond to a person who

uses the dog's name followed by "Where are you?" In one instance, for example, a woman has a 10-year-old companion dog who went blind, but who never fails to locate her owner when asked, "Where are you?"

Children particularly love to play this game with their dogs. Children can hide in smaller places like a shower or bathtub, behind a bed or under a table. The dog needs to work a little bit harder to find these hiding places but, when he does, he loves to celebrate with a treat and a tussle with a favorite youngster.

TEACHING HEEL

Heeling means that the dog walks beside the owner without pulling. It takes time and patience on the owner's part to succeed at teaching the dog that he (the owner) will not proceed unless the dog is walking calmly beside him. Pulling out ahead on the leash is definitely not acceptable.

Begin with holding the leash in your left hand as the dog sits beside your left leg. Hold the loop end of the leash in your right hand but keep your left hand short on the leash so it keeps the dog in close next to you.

Say "Heel" and step forward on your left foot. Keep the dog close to you and take three steps. Stop and have the dog sit next to you in what we now call the heel position. Praise verbally, but do

Many dogs respond better to their name and a short expression like "Where are you?"

TUG OF WALK?

If you begin teaching the heel by taking long walks and letting the dog pull you along, he misinterprets this action as an acceptable form of taking a walk. When you pull back on the lead to counteract his pulling, he reads that tug as a signal to pull even harder!

not touch the dog. Hesitate a moment and begin again with "Heel," taking three steps and stopping, at which point the dog is told to sit again.

Your goal here is to have the dog walk those three steps without pulling on the leash. When he will walk calmly beside you for three steps without pulling, increase the number of steps you take to five. When he will walk politely beside you while you take five steps, you can increase the length of your walk to ten steps. Keep increasing the length of your stroll until the dog will walk quietly beside you without pulling as long as you want him to heel. When you stop heeling, indicate to the dog that the exercise is over by verbally praising as you pet him and say "OK, good dog." The "OK" is used as a release word, meaning that the exercise is finished and the dog is free to relax.

If you are dealing with a dog who insists on pulling you around, simply "put on your brakes" and stand your ground until the dog realizes that the two of you are not going anywhere until he is beside you and moving at your pace, not his. It may take some time just standing there to convince the dog that you are the leader and you will be the one to decide on the direction and speed of your travel.

Each time the dog looks up at you or slows down to give a slack leash between the two of you, quietly praise him and say, "Good heel. Good dog." Eventually, the dog will begin to respond and within a few days he will be walking politely beside you without pulling on the leash. At first, the training sessions should be kept

Walking your Boxer will be unpleasant for both of you if he pulls or behaves poorly on the leash.

short and very positive; soon the dog will be able to walk nicely with you for increasingly longer distances. Remember also to give the dog free time and the opportunity to run and play when you are done with heel practice.

WEANING OFF FOOD IN TRAINING

Food is used in training new behaviors, yet once the dog understands what behavior goes with a specific command, it is time to start weaning him off the food treats. At first, give a treat after each exercise. Then, start to give a treat only after every other exercise. Vary the times when you offer a food reward and the times when you only offer praise so that the dog will never know when he is going to receive both food and praise and when he is going to receive only praise. This is called a variable ratio reward system and it proves successful because there is always the chance that the owner will produce a treat, so the dog never stops trying for that reward. No matter what, *always* give verbal praise.

OBEDIENCE CLASSES

As previously discussed, it is a good idea to enroll in an obedience class if one is available in your area. Many areas have dog clubs that offer basic obedience training as well as preparatory classes for obedience competition. There are also local dog trainers who offer similar classes.

At obedience trials, dogs can earn titles at various levels of competition. The beginning levels of competition include basic behaviors such as sit, down, heel, etc. The more advanced levels of competition include jumping, retrieving, scent discrimination and signal work. The advanced levels require a dog and owner to put a lot of time and effort into their training; the titles that can be earned at these levels of competition are very prestigious.

OTHER ACTIVITIES FOR LIFE

Whether a dog is trained in the structured environment of a class or alone with his owner at home, there are many activities that can bring fun and rewards to both owner and dog once they have mastered basic control.

Boxers excel in many competitions, including Schutzhund tests and trials. This Boxer is flying over the high jump to "assail" his sleeved opponent.

Teaching the dog to help out around the home, in the yard or on the farm provides great satisfaction to both dog and owner. In addition, the dog's help makes life a little easier for his owner and raises his stature as a valued companion to his family. It helps give the dog a purpose; it helps to keep his mind occupied and provides an outlet for his energy.

Backpacking is an exciting and healthful activity that the dog can be taught without assistance from more than his owner. The exercise of walking and climbing is good for man and dog alike, and the bond that they develop together is priceless.

If you are interested in participating in organized competition with your Boxer, there are activities other than obedience in which you and your dog can become involved. Agility is a popular and fun sport where dogs run through an obstacle course that includes various jumps, tunnels and other exercises to test the dog's speed and coordination. The owners run through the course beside their dogs to give commands and to guide them through the course. Although competitive, the focus is on fun— it's fun to do and fun to watch, as well as great exercise.

As a Boxer owner, you have the opportunity to participate in Schutzhund competition if you choose. Schutzhund originated in

Germany as a test to determine the best quality Boxers to be used for breeding stock. It is now used as a way to evaluate working ability and temperament, and some Boxer owners choose to train and compete with their dogs in Schutzhund trials. There are three levels of Schutzhund, SchH. I, SchH. II and SchH. III, each level being progressively more difficult to complete successfully. Each level consists of training, obedience and protection phases. Training for Schutzhund is intense and must be practiced consistently to keep the dog keen. The experience of Schutzhund training is very rewarding for dog and owner, and the Boxer's tractability is well suited for this type of training.

Boxers are very intelligent dogs. When properly maintained and exercised, they can perform many feats of physical splendor.

Health Care of Your Boxer

Dogs, being mammals like human beings, suffer from many of the same physical illnesses as people. They might even share many of the psychological problems. Since people usually know more about human diseases than canine maladies, many of the terms used in this chapter will be the familiar terms, not necessarily those used by veterinarians. We'll still use the term *x-ray*, instead of the more acceptable term *radiograph*. We will also use the familiar term *symptoms* even though dogs don't have symptoms; they have *clinical signs*.

Symptoms, by the way, are verbal descriptions of the patient's feelings. Since dogs can't speak, we have to look for clinical signs...but we still use the term *symptoms* in this book.

As a general rule, medicine is *practiced*. That term is not arbitrary. Medicine is a constantly changing art as we learn more and more about genetics, electronic aids (like CAT scans and MRIs) and new opinions. There are many dog maladies, like canine hip dysplasia, which are not universally treated in the same manner. Some vets opt for surgery more often than others.

You have a responsibility to your Boxer to keep him healthy. Regular visits to your vet will inhibit debilitating diseases and keep your dog free of parasites, both internal and external.

SELECTING A QUALIFIED VET

Your selection of a veterinarian should be based not only upon his personality and ability with large-breed dogs but also upon his convenience to your home. You want a vet who is close, as you might have emergencies or need multiple visits for treatments. You want a vet who has services that you might require such as a boarding kennel or grooming facilities, who makes sophisticated pet supplies available and who has a good reputation for ability and responsiveness. There is nothing more frustrating than having to wait a day or more to get a response from a vet.

All veterinarians are licensed and their diplomas and/or certificates should be displayed in their waiting rooms. There are, however, many veterinary specialties that usually require further studies and internships. There are specialists in heart problems (veterinary cardiologists), skin problems (veterinary dermatologists), teeth and gum problems (veterinary dentists), eye problems (veterinary ophthalmologists) and x-rays (veterinary radiologists), and vets who have specialties in bones, muscles or certain organs. Most vets do routine surgery such as neutering, stitching up wounds and docking tails for those breeds in which such is required

Your veterinarian can easily become your dog's most valuable friend, next to you, of course!

for show purposes. When the problem affecting your dog is serious, it is not unusual or impudent to get another medical opinion. You might also want to compare costs between several veterinarians. Sophisticated health care and veterinary services can be very costly. Don't be bashful about discussing these costs with your vet or his staff. It is not infrequent that important decisions are based upon financial considerations.

PREVENTATIVE MEDICINE

It is much easier, less costly and more effective to practice preventative medicine than to fight bouts of illness and disease. Properly bred puppies come from parents that were selected based upon their genetic-disease profiles. Their mother should have been vaccinated, free of all internal and external parasites and properly nourished. For these reasons, a visit to the vet who cared for the dam is recommended. The dam can pass on disease resistance to her puppies. This resistance can last for eight to ten weeks. She can also pass on parasites and many infections. That's why you should learn as much about the dam's health as possible.

WEANING TO FIVE MONTHS OLD

Puppies should be weaned by the time they are about two months old. A puppy that remains for at least eight weeks with his mother and littermates usually adapts better to other dogs and people later in life.

In every case, you should have your newly acquired puppy examined by a vet as soon as

CARING FOR MOM

Caring for the puppy starts before the puppy is born by keeping the dam healthy and well-nourished. When the puppy is about three weeks old, it must start its disease-control regimen. The first treatments will be for worms. Most puppies have worms, even if they are tested negative for worms. The test essentially is checking the stool specimens for the eggs of the worms. The worms continually shed eggs except during their dormant stage when they just rest in the tissues of the puppy. During this stage they don't shed eggs and are not evident during a routine examination.

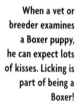

When a vet or breeder examines a Boxer puppy, he can expect lots of kisses. Licking is part of being a Boxer!

possible. Vaccination programs usually begin when the puppy is around six weeks of age, so you will need to continue this.

The puppy will have his teeth examined, his skeletal conformation checked and his general health checked prior to certification by the vet. Many puppies have problems with their knee caps, cataracts and

HEALTH AND VACCINATION SCHEDULE

AGE IN WEEKS:	3RD	6TH	8TH	10TH	12TH	14TH	16TH	52ND
Worm Control	✔	✔	✔	✔	✔	✔	✔	✔
Neutering								✔
Heartworm		✔						✔
Parvovirus		✔		✔		✔		✔
Distemper		✔		✔		✔		
Hepatitis		✔		✔		✔		
Leptospirosis		✔		✔		✔		
Parainfluenza		✔		✔		✔		
Dental Examination			✔					✔
Complete Physical			✔					✔
Temperament Testing			✔					
Coronavirus					✔			
Canine Cough		✔						
Hip Dysplasia							✔	
Rabies								✔

Vaccinations are not instantly effective. It takes about two weeks for the dog's immune system to develop antibodies. Most vaccinations require annual booster shots. Your vet should guide you in this regard.

other eye problems, heart murmurs and undescended testicles. Your veterinarian might also have training in temperament evaluation.

VACCINATION SCHEDULING
Vaccinations should only be administered by a veterinarian. Both he and you should keep a record of the date of the injection, the identification of the vaccine and the amount given. The vaccination scheduling is based on a 15-day cycle. The first vaccinations should start when the puppy is 6–8 weeks old, then 15 days later when he is 10–12 weeks of age and later when he is 14–16 weeks of age. Vaccinations should *never* be given without a 15-day lapse between injections. Most vaccinations immunize your puppy against viruses.

The usual vaccines contain immunizing doses of several different viruses such as distemper, parvovirus, parainfluenza and hepatitis. There are other vaccines available when the puppy is at risk. You should rely upon professional advice. This is especially true for the booster-

DENTAL HEALTH

A dental examination is in order when the dog is between six months and one year of age so that any permanent teeth that have erupted incorrectly can be corrected. It is important to begin a brushing routine at home, using dental-care products made for dogs, like canine toothbrushes and specially formulated toothpaste. Durable nylon and safe edible chews should be a part of your Boxer's arsenal for good health, good teeth and pleasant breath. The vast majority of dogs three to four years old and older has diseases of the gums from lack of dental attention. Using the various types of dental chews can be very effective in controlling dental plaque.

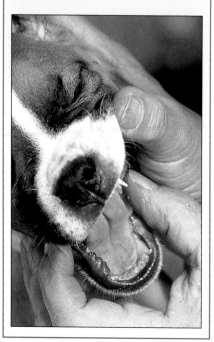

shot program. Most vaccination programs require a booster when the puppy is a year old, and once a year thereafter. In some cases, circumstances may require more frequent immunizations.

Kennel or canine cough, more formally known as tracheo-bronchitis, is treated with a vaccine which is sprayed into the dog's nostrils.

The effectiveness of a parvovirus vaccination program can be tested to be certain that the vaccinations are protective. Your veterinarian will explain and manage all of these details.

FIVE MONTHS TO ONE YEAR OF AGE

By the time your puppy is five months old, he should have completed his vaccination program. During his physical examination he should be evaluated for the common hip dysplasia plus other diseases of the joints. There are tests to assist in the prediction of these problems. Other tests can also be run, such as the parvovirus antibody titer, which can assess the effectiveness of the vaccination program.

Unless you intend to breed or show your dog, neutering the puppy at six months of age is recommended. Discuss this with your veterinarian. If the puppy is not a show dog or a candidate for a breeding program, most professionals advise neutering the puppy. Neutering/spaying

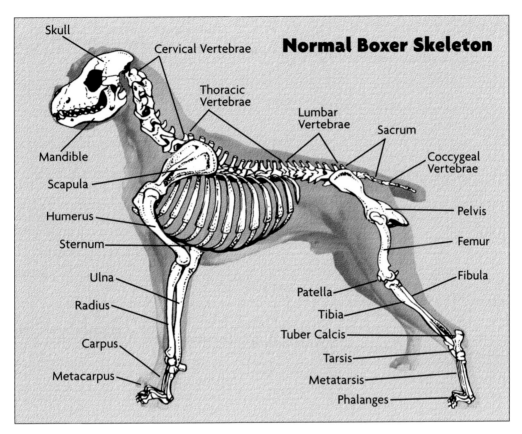

Normal Boxer Skeleton

Skull
Cervical Vertebrae
Thoracic Vertebrae
Lumbar Vertebrae
Sacrum
Coccygeal Vertebrae
Mandible
Scapula
Humerus
Sternum
Ulna
Radius
Carpus
Metacarpus
Pelvis
Femur
Fibula
Patella
Tibia
Tuber Calcis
Tarsis
Metatarsis
Phalanges

has proven to be extremely beneficial to both male and female puppies. Besides the obvious impossibility of pregnancy, these procedures inhibit (but do not prevent) breast cancer in bitches and prostate cancer in male dogs.

Discuss heartworm preventatives with you veterinarian. Blood tests must be performed for heartworm infestation and it is possible that your puppy will be placed on a preventative therapy, which will prevent heartworm infection as well as control other internal parasites.

DOGS OLDER THAN ONE YEAR
Continue to visit the vet at least once a year. There is no such disease as old age, but bodily functions do change with age, and the eyes and ears become less efficient, as do the internal workings of the liver, kidneys and intestines. Proper dietary changes, recommended by your vet, can make life more pleasant for the aging Boxer and you.

BREED-SPECIFIC HEALTH PROBLEMS

Unfortunately, there are too many conditions that appear to be prominent in our breed, though the dedication and knowledge of breeders have limited the occurrence of many of these illnesses. For your sake, and the sake of the puppy that you purchase, be certain that the breeder has done his homework. Screening for the various congenital defects is the first step to ensuring a longer life for the Boxers around us. Breeders who do not feel it is necessary to test their stock are the breeders you want to avoid. Don't let a smooth-talking breeder convince

Disease	What is it?	What causes it?	Symptoms
Leptospirosis	Severe disease that affects the internal organs; can be spread to people.	A bacterium, which is often carried by rodents, that enters through mucous membranes and spreads quickly throughout the body.	Range from fever, vomiting and loss of appetite in less severe cases to shock, irreversible kidney damage and possibly death in most severe cases.
Rabies	Potentially deadly virus that infects warm-blooded mammals.	Bite from a carrier of the virus, mainly wild animals.	1st stage: dog exhibits change in behavior, fear. 2nd stage: dog's behavior becomes more aggressive. 3rd stage: loss of coordination, trouble with bodily functions.
Parvovirus	Highly contagious virus, potentially deadly.	Ingestion of the virus, which is usually spread through the feces of infected dogs.	Most common: severe diarrhea. Also vomiting, fatigue, lack of appetite.
Kennel or canine cough	Contagious respiratory infection.	Combination of types of bacteria and virus. Most common: *Bordetella bronchiseptica* bacteria and parainfluenza virus.	Chronic cough.
Distemper	Disease primarily affecting respiratory and nervous system.	Virus that is related to the human measles virus.	Mild symptoms such as fever, lack of appetite and mucus secretion progress to evidence of brain damage, "hard pad."
Hepatitis	Virus primarily affecting the liver.	Canine adenovirus type I (CAV-1). Enters system when dog breathes in particles.	Lesser symptoms include listlessness, diarrhea, vomiting. More severe symptoms include "blue-eye" (clumps of virus in eye).
Coronavirus	Virus resulting in digestive problems.	Virus is spread through infected dog's feces.	Stomach upset evidenced by lack of appetite, vomiting, diarrhea.

you that his stock is unique and that he has never encountered any problems with his Boxers. What this breeder is really saying is, "I don't recognize any of those problems" and "I haven't screened any of my dogs."

The second step toward a healthy Boxer is your knowledge of the conditions that may affect the Boxer. There are early warning signs in many of these conditions and you should always keep a close eye on your dog.

Perhaps the most disheartening disease that Boxer breeders and owners must contend with is cancer, which of course comes in many forms. Breeders must screen their stock for cancers, though it is difficult to be certain since so much about cancer is still being learned. The breed can be prone to both malignant and benign forms; the most common form of malignant cancer is a mast-cell tumor.

The second condition that Boxers suffer from concerns the heart. The defect known as dilated cardiomyopathy, affecting the heart muscles, causes heart failure in Boxers. Like a balloon, the muscles of the heart become thin and stretched, keeping the heart from functioning properly and pumping blood efficiently. Although cardiomyopathy affects other breeds, in

Your Boxer's health is directly related to the care you give him. Regular veterinary check-ups are a requirement for a sound health care program.

Boxers its genetic predisposition is likely dominant; thereby making it essential for Boxer breeders to screen their stock before breeding. Owners should keep their eyes out for early warning signs that might include general weakness, difficulty breathing, moping, coughing, difficulty with vigorous activity, lack or loss of appetite, increased heart rate and maybe fainting. Veterinary examinations are essential, because in worst-case scenarios there are no signs. This is especially true with our breed. Dilated cardiomyopathy can be positively identified by your vet, and although there is no cure presently, many Boxers respond well to therapies that include dietary supplements.

Less prevalent in the breed is aortic stenosis, another heart condition that involves the aortic valve and its obstruction. It affects young puppies and is genetically transmitted in Boxers.

Bloat claims more lives of Boxers than anyone would like to admit. In fact, pure-bred dogs in general are three or four times as likely to be affected than are mongrels. This condition, which nevertheless is not believed to be congenital, occurs in deep-chested dogs like the Boxer. Gastric torsion, dilatation or volvulus, as bloat is called by veterinarians, refers to the condition in which the stomach fills up with air (which the dog swallows). The stomach then twists, blocking the flow of food, blood, etc., from entering or exiting the organ, and often causing death as toxins are released into the dog's bloodstream. Approximately one-third of the dogs that suffer from bloat do not recover.

While the condition is never entirely avoidable, there are a number of precautions owners can take to protect their Boxers from bloat. Feed your adult Boxer in three smaller meals per day instead of one large meal, which the dog would have the tendency to gobble up. It is in the gulping of food (and air) that air is swallowed to cause bloat. Some vets recommend adding squeaky toys or chew bones to the dog's bowl so that the dog has to eat around them, and therefore never gulps his food (or

DETECTING BLOAT

As important as it is to take precautions against bloat/gastric torsion, it is of equal importance to recognize the symptoms. It is necessary for your Boxer to get immediate veterinary attention if you notice any of the following signs:

- Your dog's stomach starts to distend, ending up large and as tight as a football;
- Your dog is dribbling, as no saliva can be swallowed;
- Your dog makes frequent attempts to vomit but cannot bring anything up due to the stomach's being closed off;
- Your dog is distressed from pain;
- Your dog starts to suffer from clinical shock, meaning that there is not enough blood in the dog's circulation as the hard, dilated stomach stops the blood from returning to the heart to be pumped around the body. Clinical shock is indicated by pale gums and tongue, as they have been starved of blood. The shocked dog also has glazed, staring eyes.

You have minutes, yes minutes, to get your dog into surgery. If you see any of these symptoms at any time of the day or night, get to the vet immediately. Someone will have to phone and warn that you are on your way (which is a justification for the invention of the cellular phone!), so that they can be prepared to get your pet on the operating table.

Some Boxers, unfortunately, suffer from cancer. Their second most serious condition is heart disease. Only your vet can accurately diagnose these ailments.

water). Add water to dry kibble, and have water available during the day but never at mealtimes. Like the rule your mother told you about swimming as a child, do not let the dog exercise for at least one hour before or after he eats. Use a bowl stand to lift your dog's food so that he does not have to stretch his neck to the floor to eat. Make sure the dog is calm at mealtime. If you observe these simple daily precautions, your Boxer has a better chance of a long, happy, bloat-free life.

As with most other medium-to large-sized dogs, Boxers are prone to joint and skeletal problems, the most common being hip dysplasia. While many Boxers are genetically susceptible to hip dysplasia, not all dogs will show signs of it. Breeders commonly have a dog x-rayed at two years of age, before they are bred, to determine the quality of the dog's hips. Hip dysplasia is not merely a cosmetic smear, a condition that affects the gait of show dogs; it is a serious, crippling disease that can render a beloved pet wracked with pain and lame. Consider how vigorously your Boxer loves to play and jump! Now imagine that every step he takes causes sharp pain throughout his body. No one wants to see his dog unable to run without discomfort. Today there are simply too many irresponsibly bred dogs, dogs

DO YOU KNOW ABOUT HIP DYSPLASIA?

Hip dysplasia is a fairly common condition found in Boxers, as well as other breeds. When a dog has hip dysplasia, his hind leg has an incorrectly formed hip joint. By constant use of the hip joint, it becomes more and more loose, wears abnormally and may become arthritic.

Hip dysplasia can only be confirmed with an x-ray, but certain symptoms may indicate a problem. Your Boxer may have a hip dysplasia problem if he walks in a peculiar manner, hops instead of smoothly running, uses his hinds legs in unison (to keep the pressure off the weak joint), has trouble getting up from a prone position and always sits with both legs together on one side of his body. As the dog matures, he may adapt well to life with a bad hip, but in a few years the arthritis develops and many Boxers with hip dysplasia become crippled. Hip dysplasia is considered an inherited disease and can usually be predicted when the dog is three to nine months old.

Some experts claim that a special diet might help your puppy outgrow the bad hip, but the usual treatments are surgical. The removal of the pectineus muscle, the removal of the round part of the femur, reconstructing the pelvis and replacing the hip with an artificial one. All of these surgical interventions are expensive, but they are usually very successful. Follow the advice of your veterinarian.

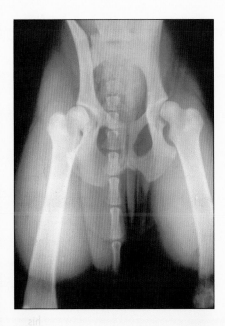

Compare the two hip joints and you'll understand dysplasia better. Hip dysplasia is a badly worn hip joint caused by improper fit of the bone into the socket. It is easily the most common hip problem in dogs. Left: X-ray of "moderate" dysplastic hips. Below left: X-ray of "good" hips.

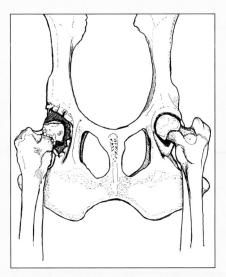

The healthy hip joint on the right and the unhealthy hip joint on the left.

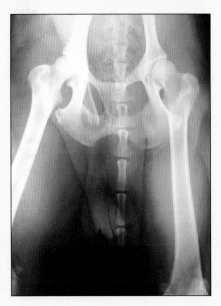

Hip dysplasia can only be positively diagnosed by x-ray. Boxers manifest the problem when they are between four and nine months of age, the so-called fast growth period, although a dog cannot be determined to be clear of hip dysplasia until he is two years old.

whose parents were not screened for dysplasia, who can barely keep up with their owners while walking through the park.

A similar form of dysplasia concerns the elbows, which affects dogs quite suddenly, rendering them lame. Arthritis usually results in the elbow joints from the complex of disorders that veterinarians call elbow dysplasia. As with hip dysplasia, the dogs are x-rayed for elbow dysplasia. Only dogs that have "normal" elbows should be used for breeding purposes.

The bleeding disorder known as von Willebrand's disease affects many pure-bred dogs, including the Boxer. This is an inherited disorder that is believed to be associated with hypothyroidism. While the incidence of von Willebrand's disease has been on the rise in recent years, there are ways of determining the amount of the vW factor in the blood.

Elbow dysplasia in a three-and-a-half-year-old dog.

> ## PARVO FOR THE COURSE
> Canine parvovirus is a highly contagious disease that attacks puppies and older dogs. Spread through contact with infected feces, parvovirus causes bloody diarrhea, vomiting, heart damage, dehydration, shock and death. To prevent this tragedy, have your puppy begin his series of vaccinations at six to eight weeks of age. Be aware that the virus is easily spread and is carried on a dog's hair, feet, water bowls and other objects, as well as on people's shoes and clothing.

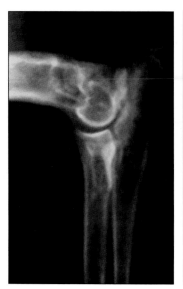
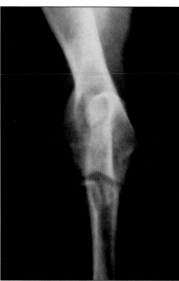
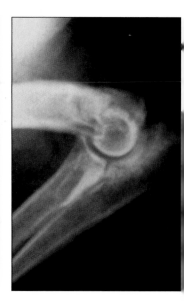

Hypothyroidism, a hormonal problem that is fairly common in Boxers, usually shows up in mature dogs, usually no earlier than five years of age. There are few early signs that an owner would recognize, though lethargy and recurrent illness or infection have been cited, as has loss of hair. Obesity, often thought to be the most common manifestation, is seen in very few cases. Although the diagnosis of hypothyroidism is tricky, vets can treat the disease rather easily and the expense incurred is not great.

In the early 1980s, England's Boxer population was scourged by progressive axonopathy, an inherited nerve disorder that is seen exclusively in our breed. Thanks to the expertise of animal geneticist Dr. Bruce Cattanach, the mode of inheritance of PA was confirmed. Breeders in England, responsibly breeding away from affected dogs, have completely eradicated the breed from PA. The disease is characterized by awkward rear movement in young pups, usually six months of age, which eventually progresses to the forequarters. Although both parents must carry the genes for PA for the pups to be affected, any carrier dog or its progeny should not be bred. The disease is not a problem in North America.

Another disease that affects the Boxer almost exclusively is known as histiocytic ulcerative colitis. Affecting young dogs less than two years old, this inflammatory disorder of the bowels is marked by diarrhea and similar signs of colitis. A combination of antibiotics and diet helps to ease sufferers, though there is no cure and the condition is chronic. Since a genetic link is suspected by vets, affected dogs are not to be bred.

There are far too many hereditary conditions that affect the Boxer to describe here. Discuss any of the mentioned diseases with your veterinarian and your breeder. Responsible breeders know their lines in and

A SKUNKY PROBLEM
Have you noticed your dog dragging his rump along the floor? If so, it is likely that his anal sacs are impacted or possibly infected. The anal sacs are small pouches located on both sides of the anus under the skin and muscles. They are about the size and shape of a grape and contain a foul-smelling liquid. Their contents are usually emptied when the dog has a bowel movement but, if not emptied completely, they will impact, which will cause your dog much pain. Fortunately, your veterinarian can tend to this problem easily by draining the sacs for the dog. Be aware that your dog might also empty his anal sacs in cases of extreme fright.

out and should be able to allay your fears of the possibilities of any of these conditions in your puppy. Among the other conditions that vets recommend Boxer folk should look out for are Cushing's syndrome, corneal ulcers, distichiasis, entropion, lymphosarcoma and pulmonic stenosis.

SKIN PROBLEMS IN BOXERS
Vets are consulted by dog owners for skin problems more than for any other group of diseases or maladies. Dogs' skin is almost as sensitive as human skin and both suffer almost the same ailments (though the occurrence of acne in dogs is rare). For this reason, veterinary dermatology has developed into a specialty practiced by many veterinarians.

Since many skin problems have visual symptoms that are

Responsible breeders screen their breeding stock before planning a litter. This pair of puppies were bred by top breeders in Australia.

almost identical, it requires the skill of an experienced veterinary dermatologist to identify and cure many of the more severe skin disorders. Pet shops sell many treatments for skin problems, but most of the treatments are simply directed at symptoms and not the underlying problem(s). Simply put, if your dog is suffering from a skin disorder, seek professional assistance as quickly as possible. As with all diseases, the earlier a problem is identified and treated, the more likely is the cure.

HEREDITARY SKIN DISORDERS
Veterinary dermatologists are currently researching a number of skin disorders that are believed to have a hereditary basis. These inherited diseases are transmitted by both parents, who appear (phenotypically) normal but have a recessive gene for the disease, meaning that they carry but are not affected by the disease. These diseases pose serious problems to breeders because in some instances there are no methods of identifying carriers. Often the secondary diseases associated with these skin conditions are even more debilitating than the skin disorders themselves; these can include cancers and respiratory problems.

Among the hereditary skin disorders, for which the mode of

inheritance is known, are cutaneous asthenia (Ehlers-Danlos syndrome), which has been cited in the Boxer, acrodermatitis, sebaceous adenitis, cyclic hematopoiesis, dermatomyositis, IgA deficiency, color dilution alopecia and nodular dermatofibrosis. Some of these disorders are limited to one or two breeds, while others affect a large number of breeds. All inherited diseases must be diagnosed and treated by a veterinary specialist.

PARASITE BITES

Many of us are allergic to mosquito bites. The bites itch, erupt and may even become infected. Dogs have the same reaction to fleas, ticks and/or mites. When you feel the prick of the mosquito when it bites you, you have a chance to kill it with your hand. Unfortunately, when your dog is bitten by a flea, tick or mite, he can only scratch it away or bite it. By the time the dog has been bitten, the parasite has done some of its damage. It may also have laid eggs to cause further problems in the near future. The itching from parasite bites is probably due to the saliva injected into the site when the parasite sucks the dog's blood.

ACRAL LICK GRANULOMA

Boxers and other dogs about the same size (like Labrador Retriev-

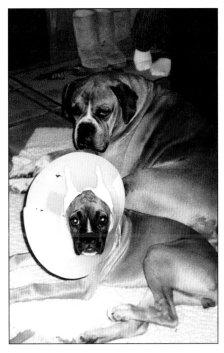

Acral lick results from the Boxer's constant licking and causing a hot spot on his leg. The collar used for a Boxer's healing ears may be helpful in treating acral lick disease by preventing access to the raw area.

ers) have a very poorly understood syndrome called *acral lick granuloma*. The manifestation of the problem is the dog's tireless attack at a specific area of the body, often the legs. The dog licks so intensively that he removes the hair and skin, leaving a large wound. There is no absolute cure, but corticosteroids are the most common treatment.

AIRBORNE PROBLEMS

Just as humans have hay fever, rose fever and other fevers from which they suffer during the pollinating season, many dogs suffer from the same allergies. Don't expect your dog to sneeze and have a runny nose like a human would. Dogs react to pollen allergies the same way they react to fleas—they scratch and bite themselves. Boxers are very susceptible to airborne pollen allergies.

Dogs, like humans, can be tested for allergens. Discuss the testing with your veterinary dermatologist.

FOOD PROBLEMS

Dogs are allergic to or intolerant of many foods that are best-sellers and highly recommended by breeders and veterinarians. Changing the brand of food that you buy may not eliminate the problem because the element of the food to which the dog is allergic may also be contained in the new brand.

Recognizing a food allergy is difficult. Humans vomit or have rashes when they eat a food to which they are allergic. Dogs neither vomit nor (usually) develop a rash. Instead they itch, scratch and bite, thus making the diagnosis extremely difficult. While pollen allergies and parasite bites are usually seasonal, food allergies and other problems are year-round occurrences.

TREATING FOOD PROBLEMS

Handling food allergies and food intolerance yourself is possible. Put your dog on a diet that he has never had. Obviously, if he has never eaten this new food, he can't yet have been allergic or intolerant of it. Start with a single ingredient which is *not* in the dog's diet at the present time. Ingredients like chopped beef or chicken are common in dog's diets, so try something like fish, lamb, rabbit or some other source of quality protein. Keep the dog on this diet (with no additives) for a month. If the symptoms of food allergy or intolerance disappear, chances are that you have defined the cause of the problem.

Don't think that the single ingredient cured the problem. You still must find a suitable diet and ascertain which ingredient in the old diet was objectionable. This is most easily done by adding ingredients to the new diet one at a time until you find the problem ingredient. Let the dog stay on the modified diet for a month before you add another ingredient.

An alternative method is to carefully study the ingredients in the diet to which your dog is allergic or intolerant. Identify the main ingredient in this diet and eliminate it by buying a different food which does not have that ingredient. Keep experimenting until the symptoms disappear after one month on the new diet.

Number-One Killer Disease in Dogs: CANCER

In every age, there is a word associated with a disease or plague that causes humans to shudder. In the 21st century, that word is "cancer." Just as cancer is the leading cause of death in humans, it claims nearly half the lives of dogs that die from a natural disease as well as half the dogs that die over the age of ten years.

Described as a genetic disease, cancer becomes a greater risk as the dog ages. Veterinarians and dog owners have become increasingly aware of the threat of cancer to dogs. Statistics reveal that one dog in every five will develop cancer, the most common of which is skin cancer. Many cancers, including prostate, ovarian and breast cancer, can be avoided by spaying and neutering our dogs by the age of six months.

Early detection of cancer can save or extend your dog's life, so it is absolutely vital for owners to have their dogs examined by a qualified veterinarian or oncologist immediately upon detection of any abnormality. Certain dietary guidelines have also proven to reduce the onset and spread of cancer. Foods based on fish rather than beef, due to the presence of Omega-3 fatty acids, are recommended. Other amino acids such as glutamine have significant benefits for canines, particularly those breeds that show a greater susceptibility to cancer.

Cancer management and treatments promise hope for future generations of canines. Since the disease is genetic, breeders should never breed a dog whose parents, grandparents and any related siblings have developed cancer. It is difficult to know whether to exclude an otherwise healthy dog from a breeding program as the disease does not manifest itself until the dog's senior years.

RECOGNIZE CANCER WARNING SIGNS

Since early detection can possibly rescue your dog from becoming a cancer statistic, it is essential for owners to recognize the possible signs and seek the assistance of a qualified professional.

- Abnormal bumps or lumps that continue to grow
- Bleeding or discharge from any body cavity
- Persistent stiffness or lameness
- Recurrent sores or sores that do not heal
- Inappetence
- Breathing difficulties
- Weight loss
- Bad breath or odors
- General malaise and fatigue
- Eating and swallowing problems
- Difficulty urinating and defecating

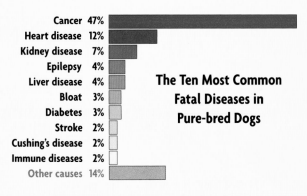

Cancer	47%
Heart disease	12%
Kidney disease	7%
Epilepsy	4%
Liver disease	4%
Bloat	3%
Diabetes	3%
Stroke	2%
Cushing's disease	2%
Immune diseases	2%
Other causes	14%

The Ten Most Common Fatal Diseases in Pure-bred Dogs

A male dog flea, *Ctenocephalides canis.*

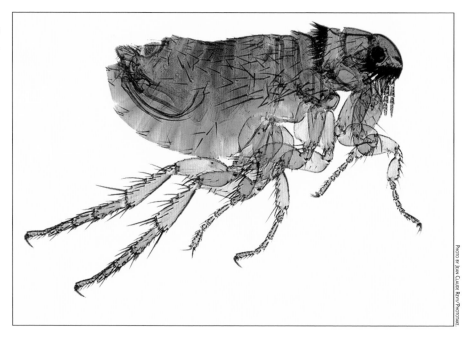

PHOTO BY JEAN CLAUDE REVY/PHOTOTAKE

EXTERNAL PARASITES

FLEAS

Of all the problems to which dogs are prone, none is more well known and frustrating than fleas. Flea infestation is relatively simple to cure but difficult to prevent. Parasites that are harbored inside the body are a bit more difficult to eradicate but they are easier to control.

To control flea infestation, you have to understand the flea's life cycle. Fleas are often thought of as a summertime problem, but centrally heated homes have changed the patterns and fleas can be found at any time of the year. The most effective method of flea control is a two-stage approach: one stage to kill the adult fleas, and the other to control the development of pre-adult fleas. Unfortunately, no single active ingredient is effective against all stages of the life cycle.

FLEA KILLER CAUTION— "POISON"

Flea-killers are poisonous. You should not spray these toxic chemicals on areas of a dog's body that he licks, including his genitals and his face. Flea killers taken internally are a better answer, but check with your vet in case internal therapy is not advised for your dog.

LIFE CYCLE STAGES

During its life, a flea will pass through four life stages: egg, larva, pupa or nymph and adult. The adult stage is the most visible and irritating stage of the flea life cycle, and this is why the majority of flea-control products concentrate on this stage. The fact is that adult fleas account for only 1% of the total flea population, and the other 99% exist in pre-adult stages, i.e., eggs, larvae and nymphs. The pre-adult stages are barely visible to the naked eye.

THE LIFE CYCLE OF THE FLEA

Eggs are laid on the dog, usually in quantities of about 20 or 30, several times a day. The adult female flea must have a blood meal before each egg-laying session. When first laid, the eggs will cling to the dog's hair, as the eggs are still moist. However, they will quickly dry out and fall from the dog, especially if the dog moves around or scratches. Many eggs will fall off in the dog's favorite area or an area in which he spends a lot of time, such as his bed.

Once the eggs fall from the dog onto the carpet or furniture, they will hatch into larvae. This takes from one to ten days. Larvae are not particularly mobile and will usually travel only a few inches from where they hatch. However, they do have a tendency to move away from bright light and heavy

EN GARDE:
CATCHING FLEAS OFF GUARD!
Consider the following ways to arm yourself against fleas:
- Add a small amount of pennyroyal or eucalyptus oil to your dog's bath. These natural remedies repel fleas.
- Supplement your dog's food with fresh garlic (minced or grated) and a hearty amount of brewer's yeast, both of which ward off fleas.
- Use a flea comb on your dog daily. Submerge fleas in a cup of bleach to kill them quickly.
- Confine the dog to only a few rooms to limit the spread of fleas in the home.
- Vacuum daily...and get all of the crevices! Dispose of the bag every few days until the problem is under control.
- Wash your dog's bedding daily. Cover cushions where your dog sleeps with towels, and wash the towels often.

traffic—under furniture and behind doors are common places to find high quantities of flea larvae.

The flea larvae feed on dead organic matter, including adult flea feces, until they are ready to change into adult fleas. Fleas will usually remain as larvae for around seven days. After this period, the larvae will pupate into protective pupae. While inside the pupae, the larvae will undergo

PHOTO BY DWIGHT R. KUHN

Fleas have been measured as being able to jump 300,000 times and can jump 150 times their length in any direction, including straight up.

metamorphosis and change into adult fleas. This can take as little time as a few days, but the adult fleas can remain inside the pupae waiting to hatch for up to two years. The pupae are signaled to hatch by certain stimuli, such as physical pressure—the pupae's being stepped on, heat from an animal's lying on the pupae or increased carbon-dioxide levels and vibrations—indicating that a suitable host is available.

Once hatched, the adult flea must feed within a few days. Once the adult flea finds a host, it will not leave voluntarily. It only becomes dislodged by grooming or the host animal's scratching.

The adult flea will remain on the host for the duration of its life unless forcibly removed.

TREATING THE ENVIRONMENT AND THE DOG

Treating fleas should be a two-pronged attack. First, the environment needs to be treated; this includes carpets and furniture, especially the dog's bedding and areas underneath furniture. The environment should be treated with a household spray containing an Insect Growth Regulator (IGR) and an insecticide to kill the adult fleas. Most IGRs are effective against eggs and larvae; they actually mimic the fleas' own hormones and stop the eggs and larvae from developing into adult fleas. There are currently no treatments available to attack the pupa stage of the life cycle, so the adult insecticide is used to kill the newly hatched adult fleas before they find a host. Most IGRs are active for many months, while

A scanning electron micrograph of a dog or cat flea, *Ctenocephalides*, magnified more than 100x. This image has been colorized for effect.

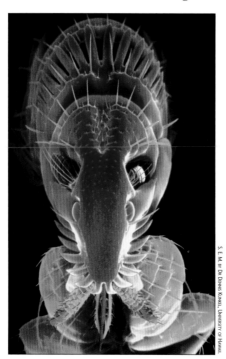

S. E. M. BY DR DENNIS KUNKEL, UNIVERSITY OF HAWAII

THE LIFE CYCLE OF THE FLEA

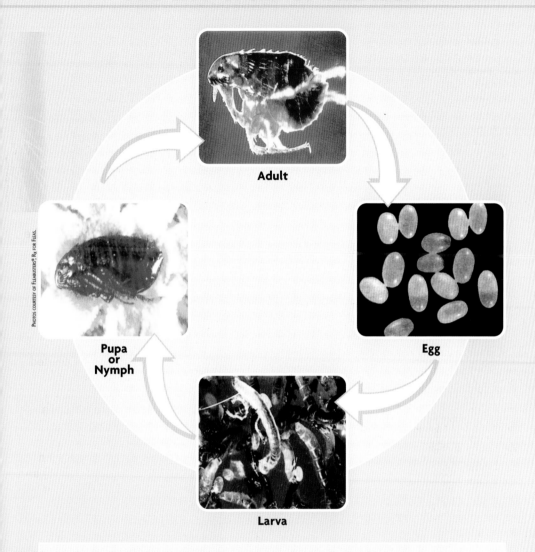

Adult

Pupa
or
Nymph

Egg

Larva

Fleas have been around for millions of years and have adapted to changing host animals. They are able to go through a complete life cycle in less than one month or they can extend their lives to almost two years by remaining as pupae or cocoons. They do not need blood or any other food for up to 20 months.

INSECT GROWTH REGULATOR (IGR)

Two types of products should be used when treating fleas—a product to treat the pet and a product to treat the home. Adult fleas represent less than 1% of the flea population. The pre-adult fleas (eggs, larvae and pupae) represent more than 99% of the flea population and are found in the environment; it is in the case of pre-adult fleas that products containing an Insect Growth Regulator (IGR) should be used in the home.

IGRs are a new class of compounds used to prevent the development of insects. They do not kill the insect outright, but instead use the insect's biology against it to stop it from completing its growth. Products that contain methoprene are the world's first and leading IGRs. Used to control fleas and other insects, this type of IGR will stop flea larvae from developing and protect the house for up to seven months.

The American dog tick, *Dermacentor variabilis*, is probably the most common tick found on dogs. Look at the strength in its eight legs! No wonder it's hard to detach them.

The second stage of treatment is to apply an adult insecticide to the dog. Traditionally, this would be in the form of a collar or a spray, but more recent innovations include digestible insecticides that poison the fleas when they ingest the dog's blood. Alternatively, there are drops that, when placed on the back of the dog's neck, spread throughout the hair and skin to kill adult fleas.

TICKS

Though not as common as fleas, ticks are found all over the tropical and temperate world. They don't bite, like fleas; they harpoon. They dig their sharp proboscis (nose) into the dog's skin and drink the blood. Their

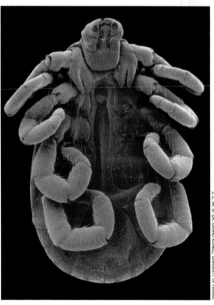

adult insecticides are only active for a few days.

When treating with a household spray, it is a good idea to vacuum before applying the product. This stimulates as many pupae as possible to hatch into adult fleas. The vacuum cleaner should also be treated with an insecticide to prevent the eggs and larvae that have been collected in the vacuum bag from hatching.

only food and drink is dog's blood. Dogs can get Lyme disease, Rocky Mountain spotted fever, tick bite paralysis and many other diseases from ticks. They may live where fleas are found and they like to hide in cracks or seams in walls. They are controlled the same way fleas are controlled.

The American dog tick, *Dermacentor variabilis*, may well be the most common dog tick in many geographical areas, especially those areas where the climate is hot and humid. Most dog ticks have life expectancies of a week to six months, depending upon climatic conditions. They can neither jump nor fly, but they can crawl slowly and can range up to 16 feet to reach a sleeping or unsuspecting dog.

MITES

Just as fleas and ticks can be problematic for your dog, mites can also lead to an itchy nuisance. Microscopic in size, mites are related to ticks and generally take up permanent residence on their host animal— in this case, your dog! The term *mange* refers to any infestation caused by one of the mighty mites, of which there are six varieties that concern dog owners.

Demodex mites cause a condition known as demodicosis

DEER-TICK CROSSING
The great outdoors may be fun for your dog, but it also is a home to dangerous ticks. Deer ticks carry a bacterium known as *Borrelia burgdorferi* and are most active in the autumn and spring. When infections are caught early, penicillin and tetracycline are effective antibiotics, but if left untreated the bacteria may cause neurological, kidney and cardiac problems as well as long-term trouble with walking and painful joints.

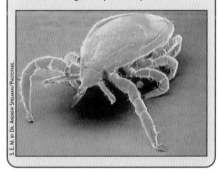

S. E. M. BY DR. ANDREW SPIELMAN/ PHOTOTAKE.

PHOTO BY DR. DENNIS KUNKEL, UNIVERSITY OF HAWAII.

The head of an American dog tick, *Dermacentor variabilis*, enlarged and colorized for effect.

The mange mite, *Psoroptes bovis*, can infest cattle and other domestic animals.

(sometimes called red mange or follicular mange), in which the mites live in the dog's hair follicles and sebaceous glands in larger-than-normal amounts. This type of mange is commonly passed from the dam to her puppies and usually shows up on the puppies' muzzles, though demodicosis is not transferable from one normal dog to another. Most dogs recover from this type of mange without any treatment, though topical therapies are commonly prescribed by the vet.

The *Cheyletiellosis* mite is the hook-mouthed culprit associated with "walking dandruff," a scondition that affects dogs as well as cats and rabbits. This mite lives on the surface of the animal's skin and is readily transferable through direct or indirect contact with an affected animal. The dandruff is present in the form of scaly skin, which may or may not be itchy. If not treated, this mange can affect a whole kennel of dogs and can be spread to humans as well.

The *Sarcoptes* mite causes intense itching on the dog in the form of a condition known as scabies or sarcoptic mange. The cycle of the *Sarcoptes* mite lasts about three weeks, and the mites live in the top layer of the dog's skin (epidermis), preferably in

Human lice look like dog lice; the two are closely related.

areas with little hair. Scabies is highly contagious and can be passed to humans. Sometimes an allergic reaction to the mite worsens the severe itching associated with sarcoptic mange.

Ear mites, *Otodectes cynotis,* lead to otodectic mange, which most commonly affects the outer ear canal of the dog, though other areas can be affected as well. Dogs with ear-mite infestation commonly scratch at their ears, causing further irritation, and shake their heads. Dark brown droppings in the outer ear confirm the diagnosis. Your vet can prescribe a treatment to flush out the ears and kill any eggs in the ears. A complete month of treatment is necessary to cure the mange.

Two other mites, less common in dogs, include *Dermanyssus gallinae* (the poultry or red mite) and *Eutrombicula alfreddugesi* (the North American mite associated with trombiculidiasis or chigger infestation). The poultry mite frequently lives on chickens, but can transfer to dogs who spend time near farm animals. Chigger infestation affects dogs in the

NOT A DROP TO DRINK
Never allow your dog to swim in polluted water or public areas where water quality can be suspect. Even perfectly clear water can harbor parasites, many of which can cause serious to fatal illnesses in canines. Areas inhabited by water-fowl and other wildlife are especially dangerous.

Central US who have exposure sto woodlands. The types of mange caused by both of these mites are treatable by veterinarians.

INTERNAL PARASITES
Most animals—fishes, birds and mammals, including dogs and humans—have worms and other parasites that live inside their bodies. According to Dr. Herbert R. Axelrod, the fish pathologist, there are two kinds of parasites: dumb and smart. The smart parasites live in peaceful cooperation with their hosts (symbiosis), while the dumb parasites kill their hosts. Most worm infections are relatively easy to control. If they are not controlled, they weaken the host dog to the point that other medical problems occur, but they do not kill the host as dumb parasites would.

A brown dog tick, *Rhipicephalus sanguineus,* is an uncommon but annoying tick found on dogs.
PHOTO BY CAROLINA BIOLOGICAL SUPPLY/PHOTOTAKE.

DO NOT MIX
Never mix parasite-control products without first consulting your vet. Some products can become toxic when combined with others and can cause fatal consequences.

The roundworm *Rhabditis* can infect both dogs and humans.

ROUNDWORMS

Average-size dogs can pass 1,360,000 roundworm eggs every day. For example, if there were only 1 million dogs in the world, the world would be saturated with thousands of tons of dog feces. These feces would contain around 15,000,000,000 roundworm eggs.

Up to 31% of home yards and children's sand boxes in the US contain roundworm eggs.

Flushing dog's feces down the toilet is not a safe practice because the usual sewage treatments do not destroy roundworm eggs.

Infected puppies start shedding roundworm eggs at three weeks of age. They can be infected by their mother's milk.

The roundworm, *Ascaris lumbricoides*.

ROUNDWORMS

The roundworms that infect dogs are known scientifically as *Toxocara canis*. They live in the dog's intestines and shed eggs continually. It has been estimated that a dog produces about 6 or more ounces of feces every day. Each ounce of feces averages hundreds of thousands of roundworm eggs. There are no known areas in which dogs roam that do not contain roundworm eggs. The greatest danger of roundworms is that they infect people, too! It is wise to have your dog tested regularly for roundworms.

In young puppies, roundworms cause bloated bellies, diarrhea, coughing and vomiting, and are transmitted from the dam (through blood or milk). Affected puppies will not appear as animated as normal puppies. The worms appear spaghetti-like, measuring as long as 6 inches. Adult dogs can acquire roundworms through coprophagia (eating contaminated feces) or by killing rodents that carry roundworms.

Roundworm infection can kill puppies and cause severe problems in adults, as the hatched larvae travel to the lungs and trachea through the bloodstream. Cleanliness is the best preventative for roundworms. Always pick up after your dog and dispose of feces in appropriate receptacles.

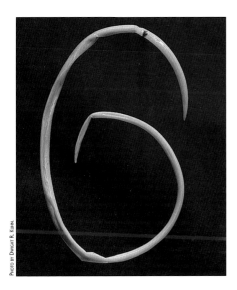

PHOTO BY DWIGHT R. KUHN

HOOKWORMS

In the United States, dog owners have to be concerned about four different species of hookworm, the most common and most serious of which is *Ancylostoma caninum,* which prefers warm climates. The others are *Ancylostoma braziliense, Ancylostoma tubaeforme* and *Uncinaria stenocephala,* the latter of which is a concern to dogs living in the Northern US and Canada, as this species prefers cold climates. Hookworms are dangerous to humans as well as to dogs and cats, and can be the cause of severe anemia due to iron deficiency. The worm uses its teeth to attach itself to the dog's intestines and changes the site of its attachment about six times per day. Each time the worm repositions itself, the dog loses

blood and can become anemic. *Ancylostoma caninum* is the most likely of the four species to cause anemia in the dog.

Symptoms of hookworm infection include dark stools, weight loss, general weakness, pale coloration and anemia, as well as possible skin problems. Fortunately, hookworms are easily purged from the affected dog with a number of medications that have proven effective. Discuss these with your veterinarian. Most heartworm preventatives include a hookworm insecticide as well.

Owners also must be aware that hookworms can infect humans, who can acquire the larvae through exposure to contaminated feces. Since the worms cannot complete their life cycle on a human, the worms simply infest the skin and cause irritation. This condition is known as cutaneous larva migrans syndrome. As a preventative, use disposable gloves or a "poop-scoop" to pick up your dog's droppings and prevent your dog (or neighborhood cats) from defecating in children's play areas.

The hookworm, *Ancylostoma caninum.*

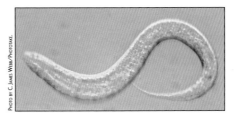

PHOTO BY C. JAMES WEBB/PHOTOTAKE.

The infective stage of the hookworm larva.

TAPEWORMS

Humans, rats, squirrels, foxes, coyotes, wolves and domestic dogs are all susceptible to tapeworm infection. Except in humans, tapeworms are usually not a fatal infection. Infected individuals can harbor 1000 parasitic worms.

Tapeworms, like some other types of worm, are hermaphroditic, meaning male and female in the same worm.

If dogs eat infected rats or mice, or anything else infected with tapeworm, they get the tapeworm disease. One month after attaching to a dog's intestine, the worm starts shedding eggs. These eggs are infective immediately. Infective eggs can live for a few months without a host animal.

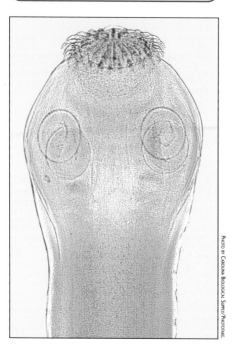

The head and rostellum (the round prominence on the scolex) of a tapeworm, which infects dogs and humans.

PHOTO BY CAROLINA BIOLOGICAL SUPPLY/PHOTOTAKE.

TAPEWORMS

There are many species of tapeworm, all of which are carried by fleas! The most common tapeworm affecting dogs is known as *Dipylidium caninum*. The dog eats the flea and starts the tapeworm cycle. Humans can also be infected with tapeworms—so don't eat fleas! Fleas are so small that your dog could pass them onto your hands, your plate or your food and thus make it possible for you to ingest a flea that is carrying tapeworm eggs.

While tapeworm infection is not life-threatening in dogs (smart parasite!), it can be the cause of a very serious liver disease for humans. About 50% of the humans infected with *Echinococcus multilocularis*, a type of tapeworm that causes alveolar hydatid, perish.

WHIPWORMS

In North America, whipworms are counted among the most common parasitic worms in dogs. The whipworm's scientific name is *Trichuris vulpis*. These worms attach themselves in the lower parts of the intestine, where they feed. Affected dogs may only experience upset tummies, colic and diarrhea. These worms, however, can live for months or years in the dog, beginning their larval stage in the small intestine, spending their adult stage in the large intestine and finally passing infective eggs through the dog's feces. The only way to detect whipworms is through a fecal examination, though this is not always foolproof. Treatment for whipworms is tricky, due to the worms' unusual life-cycle pattern, and very often dogs are reinfected due to exposure to infective eggs on the ground. The whipworm eggs can survive in the environment for as long as five years, thus cleaning up droppings in your own backyard as well as in public places is absolutely essential for sanitation purposes and the health of your dog and others.

THREADWORMS

Though less common than round-worms, hookworms and those already mentioned, threadworms concern dog owners in the South-western US and Gulf Coast area where the climate is hot and humid. Living in the small intes-tine of the dog, this worm measures a mere 2 millimeters and is round in shape. Like that of the whip-worm, the threadworm's life cycle is very complex and the eggs and larvae are passed through the feces. A deadly disease in humans, *Strongyloides* readily infects people, and the handling of feces is the most common means of trans-mission. Threadworms are most often seen in young puppies; bloody diarrhea and pneumonia are symptoms. Sick puppies must be isolated and treated immediately; vets recommend a follow-up treat-ment one month later.

HEARTWORM PREVENTATIVES

There are many heartworm preventatives on the market, many of which are sold at your veterinarian's office. These products can be given daily or monthly, depending on the manufacturer's instructions. All of these preventatives contain chemical insecticides directed at killing heartworms, which leads to some controversy among dog owners. In effect, heartworm preventatives are neces-sary evils, though you should determine how necessary based on your pet's lifestyle. There is no doubt that heartworm is a dreadful disease that threatens the lives of dogs. However, the likelihood of your dog's being bitten by an infected mosquito is slim in most places, and a mosquito-repellent (or an herbal remedy such as Wormwood or Black Walnut) is much safer for your dog and will not compromise his immune system (the way heartworm preventatives will). Should you decide to use the tradi-tional preventative "medications," you can consider giving the pill every other or third month. Since the toxins in the pill will kill the heartworms at all stages of develop-ment, the pill would be effective in killing larvae, nymphs or adults and it takes four months for the larvae to reach the adult stage. Thus, there is no rationale to poison-ing the dog's system on a monthly basis. Lastly, do not give the pill during the winter months since there are no mosquitoes around to pass on their infection, unless you live in a tropical environment.

Life Cycle of the Heartworm

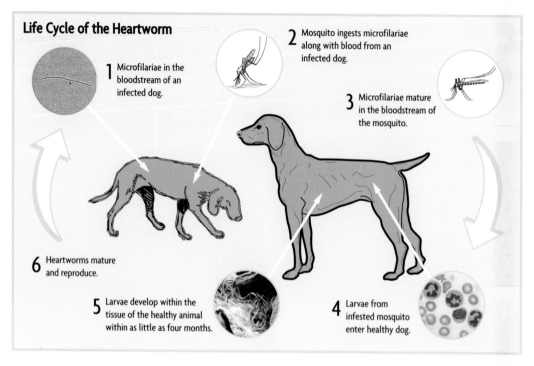

1 Microfilariae in the bloodstream of an infected dog.

2 Mosquito ingests microfilariae along with blood from an infected dog.

3 Microfilariae mature in the bloodstream of the mosquito.

6 Heartworms mature and reproduce.

5 Larvae develop within the tissue of the healthy animal within as little as four months.

4 Larvae from infested mosquito enter healthy dog.

HEARTWORMS

Heartworms are thin, extended worms up to 12 inches long, which live in a dog's heart and the major blood vessels surrounding it. Dogs may have up to 200 worms. Symptoms may be loss of energy, loss of appetite, coughing, the development of a pot belly and anemia.

Heartworms are transmitted by mosquitoes. The mosquito drinks the blood of an infected dog and takes in larvae with the blood. The larvae, called microfilariae, develop within the body of the mosquito and are passed on to the next dog bitten after the larvae mature. It takes two to three weeks for the larvae to develop to the infective stage within the body of the mosquito. Dogs are usually treated at about six weeks of age and maintained on a prophylactic dose given monthly.

Blood testing for heartworms is not necessarily indicative of how seriously your dog is infected. Although this is a dangerous disease, it is not easy for a dog to be infected. Discuss the various preventatives with your vet, as there are many different types now available. Together you can decide on a safe course of prevention for your dog.

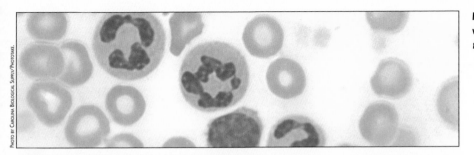

Magnified heart-
worm larvae, *Diro-
filaria immitis.*

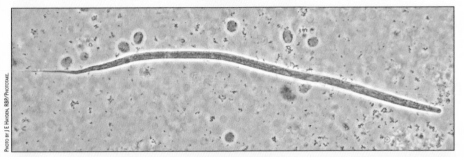

Heartworm, *Diro-
filaria immitis.*

The heart
of a dog infected
with canine heart-
worm, *Dirofilaria
immitis.*

Your Senior Boxer

The term *old* is a qualitative term. For dogs, as well as their masters, old is relative. Certainly we can all distinguish between a puppy Boxer and an adult Boxer—there are the obvious physical traits such as size and appearance, and of course, personality traits. For example, puppies and young dogs like to play with children. Children's natural exuberance is a good match for the seemingly endless energy of young dogs. They like to run, jump, chase and retrieve. When dogs grow up and cease their interaction with chil-

Older dogs still like to play and receive attention, but their physical abilities diminish as they are slowed down by age.

dren, they are often thought of as being too old to play with the kids.

On the other hand, if a Boxer is only exposed to people with quieter lifestyles, his life will normally be less active and the decrease in his energy level as he ages will not be as obvious. If people live to be 100 years old, dogs live to be 20 years old. While this is often a rule of thumb, it is *very* inaccurate. When trying to compare dog years to human years, you cannot make a generalization about all dogs. You can make the generalization that, say, 11 years is a good lifespan for a Boxer, but you cannot compare it to that of a Chihuahua, as many small breeds typically live longer than large breeds. Dogs are generally considered mature within three years. They can reproduce even earlier. So the first three years of a dog's life are similar to seven times that of comparable humans. That means a 3-year-old dog is like a 21-year-old person. However, as the curve of comparison shows, there is no hard and fast rule for comparing dog and human ages. The comparison is made even more difficult, for not all humans age at the same rate...and human females live longer than human males.

As gray begins to appear on the muzzle, old age starts to become evident.

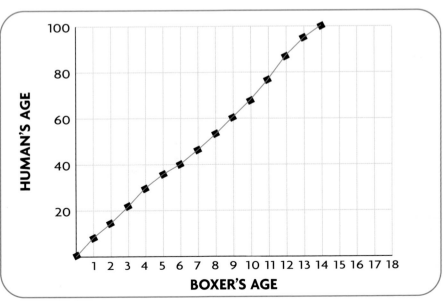

WHAT TO LOOK FOR IN SENIORS

Most veterinarians and behaviorists use the seven-year mark as the time to consider a dog a "senior." The term does not imply that the dog is geriatric and has begun to fail in mind and body. Aging is essentially a slowing process. Humans readily admit that they feel a difference in their activity level from age 20 to 30, and then from 30 to 40, etc. By treating the seven-year-old dog as a senior, owners are able to implement certain therapeutic and preventative medical strategies with the help of their veterinarians. A senior-care program should include at least two veterinary visits per year and screening sessions to determine the dog's health status, as well as nutritional counseling. Veterinarians determine the senior dog's health status through a blood smear for a complete blood count, serum chemistry profile with electrolytes, urinalysis, blood pressure check, electrocar-

NOTICING THE SYMPTOMS

The symptoms listed below are symptoms that gradually appear and become more noticeable. They are not life-threatening; however, the symptoms below are to be taken very seriously and warrant a discussion with your veterinarian:

- Your dog cries and whimpers when he moves, and he stops running completely.
- Convulsions start or become more serious and frequent. The usual convulsion (spasm) is when the dog stiffens and starts to tremble, being unable or unwilling to move. The seizure usually lasts for 5 to 30 minutes.
- Your dog drinks more water and urinates more frequently. Wetting and bowel accidents take place indoors without warning.
- Vomiting becomes more and more frequent.

diogram, ocular tonometry (pressure on the eyeball), and dental prophylaxis.

Such an extensive program for senior dogs is well advised before owners start to see the obvious physical signs of aging, such as slower and inhibited movement, graying, increased sleep/nap periods, and disinterest in play and other activity. This preventative program promises a longer, healthier life for the ageing dog. Among the physical problems common in aging dogs are the loss of sight and hearing, arthritis, kidney and liver failure, diabetes mellitus, heart disease and Cushing's disease (a hormonal disease).

In addition to the physical manifestations discussed, there are some behavioral changes and problems related to aging dogs. Dogs suffering from hearing or vision loss, dental discomfort or arthritis can become aggressive. Likewise, the near-deaf and/or blind dog may be startled more easily and react in an unexpectedly aggressive manner. Seniors suffering from senility can become more impatient and irritable. Housesoiling accidents are associated with loss of mobility, kidney problems and loss of sphincter control as well as plaque accumulation, physiological brain changes and reactions to medications. Older dogs, just like young puppies, suffer from separation anxiety, which can lead to excessive barking, whining, housesoiling, and destructive behavior. Seniors may become fearful of everyday sounds, such as vacuum cleaners, heaters, thunder and passing traffic. Some dogs have difficulty sleeping, due to discomfort, the need for frequent potty visits and the like.

Owners should avoid spoiling the older dog with too many treats. Obesity is a common problem in older dogs and subtracts years from their lives. Keep the

senior dog as trim as possible since excess weight puts additional stress on the body's vital organs. Some breeders recommend supplementing the diet with foods high in fiber and lower in calories. Adding fresh vegetables and marrow broth to the

GETTING OLD

The bottom line is simply that your dog is getting old when you think he is getting old because he slows down in his level of general activity, including walking, running, eating, jumping and retrieving. On the other hand, the frequency of certain activities increases, such as more sleeping, more barking and more repetition of habits like going to the door without being called when you put your coat on to leave the house.

senior's diet makes a tasty, low-calorie, low-fat supplement. Vets also offer specialty diets for senior dogs that are worth exploring.

Your dog, as he nears his twilight years, needs his owner's patience and good care more than ever. Never punish an older dog for an accident or abnormal behavior. For all the years of love, protection and companionship that your dog has provided, he deserves special attention and courtesies. The older dog may need to relieve himself at 3 a.m. because he can no longer hold it for eight hours. Older dogs may not be able to remain crated for more than two or three hours. It may be time to give up a couch or chair to your old friend. Although he may not seem as enthusiastic about your attention and petting, he does appreciate the considerations you offer as he gets older.

Your Boxer does not understand why his world is slowing down. Owners must make the transition into the golden years as pleasant and rewarding as possible for these dogs.

WHAT TO DO WHEN THE TIME COMES

You are never fully prepared to make a rational decision about putting your dog to sleep. It is very obvious that you love your Boxer or you would not be reading this book. Putting a loved dog to sleep is extremely difficult. It is a decision that must be made with your vet. You are usually forced to make the decision when one of the life-threatening symptoms listed above becomes serious enough for you to seek veterinary help. If the prognosis of the malady indicates the end is near and your beloved pet will only suffer more and experience no enjoyment for the balance of his life, then there is no choice but euthanasia.

WHAT IS EUTHANASIA?

Euthanasia derives from the Greek, meaning good death. In other words, it means the planned, painless killing of a dog suffering from a painful, incurable condition, or who is so aged that he cannot walk, see, eat or control his excretory functions.

Euthanasia is usually accomplished by injection with an overdose of an anesthesia or barbiturate. Aside from the prick of the needle, the experience is usually painless.

MAKING THE DECISION

The days during which the dog becomes ill and the end occurs can be unusually stressful for you. If this is your first experience with the death of a loved one, you may need the comfort dictated by your religious beliefs. If you are the head of the family and have children, you

CDS: COGNITIVE DYSFUNCTION SYNDROME
"Old-Dog Syndrome"

There are many ways to evaluate old-dog syndrome. Veterinarians have defined CDS (cognitive dysfunction syndrome) as the gradual deterioration of cognitive abilities. These are indicated by changes in the dog's behavior. When a dog changes his routine response, and maladies have been eliminated as the cause of these behavioral changes, then CDS is the usual diagnosis.

More than half the dogs over eight years old suffer from some form of CDS. The older the dog, the more chance he has of suffering from CDS. In humans, doctors often dismiss the CDS behavioral changes as part of "winding down."

There are four major signs of CDS: exhibits frequent bathroom accidents inside the home, sleeps much more or much less than normal, acts confused and fails to respond to social stimuli.

SYMPTOMS OF CDS

FREQUENT POTTY ACCIDENTS
- *Urinates in the house.*
- *Defecates in the house.*
- *Doesn't signal that he wants to go out.*

SLEEP PATTERNS
- *Takes longer to awaken.*
- *Sleeps more than normal during the day.*
- *Sleeps less during the night.*

CONFUSION
- *Goes outside and just stands there.*
- *Appears confused with a faraway look in his eyes.*
- *Hides more often.*
- *Doesn't recognize friends.*
- *Doesn't come when called.*
- *Walks around listlessly and without a destination goal.*

FAILURE TO RESPOND TO SOCIAL STIMULI
- *Comes to people less frequently, whether called or not.*
- *Doesn't tolerate petting for more than a short time.*
- *Doesn't come to the door when you return home from work.*

should have involved them in the decision of putting your Boxer to sleep. In any case, euthanasia alone is painful and stressful for the family of the dog. Unfortunately, the decision-making process is just as difficult.

Usually your dog can be maintained on drugs for a few days while he is kept in the vets clinic in order to give you ample time to make a decision. During this time, talking with members of the family or religious representatives, or even people who have lived through this same experience, can ease the burden of your inevitable decision.

THE FINAL RESTING PLACE
In terms of burials, dogs can have the same privileges as humans. They can be buried in their entirety in a pet cemetery

TALK IT OUT
The more openly your family discusses the whole stressful occurrence of the aging and eventual loss of a beloved pet, the easier it will be for you when the time comes.

in a burial container, buried in your yard in a place suitably marked with a stone or newly planted tree or bush or cremated, with the ashes being given to you.

All of these options should be discussed frankly and openly with your vet. Do not be afraid to ask financial or other questions. Cremations are usually mass burning and thus there is no way to ensure that your individual dog's ashes can be returned to you. There are very small crematoriums available to all veterinary clinics. If you

Consult your vet to help you locate a pet cemetery in your area.

Growing old together, these two senior citizens get along better than an older dog might get along with a younger one.

want a private cremation, your vet can usually arrange it. However, this may be a little more expensive.

GETTING ANOTHER DOG

The grief of losing your beloved dog will be as lasting as the grief of losing a human friend or relative. In most cases, if your dog died of old age (if there is such a thing), he had slowed down considerably. Do you want a new Boxer puppy to replace him? Or are you better off in finding a more mature Boxer, say two to three years of age, which

will usually be house-trained and will have an already developed personality.

The decision is, of course, your own. Do you want another Boxer? Perhaps you want a smaller or larger dog? Whatever you decide, do it as quickly as possible. Most people usually buy the same breed because they know (and love) the characteristics of that breed. Then, too, they often know people who have the same breed and perhaps they are lucky enough that a breeder they respect expects a litter soon. What could be better?

Showing Your Boxer

When you purchase your Boxer, you will make it clear to the breeder whether you want one just as a lovable companion and pet, or if you hope to be buying a Boxer with show prospects. No reputable breeder will sell you a young puppy and tell you that it is *definitely* of show quality, for so much can go wrong during the early months of a puppy's development. If you plan to show, what you will hopefully have acquired is a puppy with "show potential."

To the novice, exhibiting a Boxer in the show ring may look easy, but it takes a lot of hard work and devotion to do top winning at a show such as the prestigious Westminster Kennel Club dog show, not to mention a little luck too!

The first concept that the canine novice learns when watch-

ing a dog show is that each dog first competes against members of his own breed. Once the judge has selected the best member of each breed (Best of Breed), provided that the show is judged on a Group system, that chosen dog will compete with other Best of Breed dogs in his group. Finally, the dogs chosen first in each group will compete for Best in Show.

The second concept that you must understand is that the dogs are not actually compared against

Ch. Jacquet's Black Watch, Bill Scolnik's top-winning champion, is considered by many to be an exceptionally handsome dog. Breeder, Richard Tomita.

famous or popular, many dedicated enthusiasts say that a perfect specimen, as described in the standard, has never walked into a show ring, has never been bred and, to the woe of dog breeders around the globe, does not exist. Breeders attempt to get as close to this ideal as possible with every litter, but theoretically the "perfect" dog is so elusive that it is impossible. (And if the "perfect" dog were born, breeders and judges would never agree that it was indeed "perfect.")

If you are interested in exploring the world of dog showing, your best bet is to join your local breed club or the national parent club, which is the American Boxer Club. These clubs often host both regional and national specialties, shows only for Boxers, which can include conformation

one another. The judge compares each dog against his breed standard, the written description of the ideal specimen that is approved by the American Kennel Club (AKC). While some early breed standards were indeed based on specific dogs that were

PRACTICE AT HOME

If you have decided to show your dog, you must train him to gait around the ring by your side at the correct pace and pattern, and to tolerate being handled and examined by the judge. Most breeds require complete dentition, all breeds require a particular bite (scissors, level or undershot) and all males must have two apparently normal testicles fully descended into the scrotum. Enlist family and friends to hold mock trials in your yard to prepare your future champion!

English and American Ch. Jacquet's Dreams of Loriga, belonging to the Dotorovici family, is a truly magnificent specimen of the breed. Breeder, Richard Tomita.

as well as obedience and agility trials. Even if you have no intention of competing with your Boxer, a specialty is like a festival for lovers of the breed who congregate to share their favorite topic: Boxers! Clubs also send out newsletters, and some organize training days and seminars in order that people may learn more about their chosen breed. To locate the breed club closest to you, contact the American Kennel Club, which furnishes the rules and regulations for all of these events plus general dog registration and other basic requirements of dog ownership.

The American Kennel Club offers three kinds of conformation shows: an all-breed show (for all AKC-recognized breeds), a specialty show (for one breed only, usually sponsored by the parent club) and a Group show (for all breeds in the group).

For a dog to become an AKC champion of record, the dog must

The judge determines which Boxer best embodies the virtues described in the breed standard.

> **SHOW-RING ETIQUETTE**
> Just as with anything else, there is a certain etiquette to the show ring that can only be learned through experience. Showing your dog can be quite intimidating to you as a novice when it seems as if everyone else knows what he is doing. You can familiarize yourself with ring procedure beforehand by taking showing classes to prepare you and your dog for conformation showing and by talking with experienced handlers. When you are in the ring, it is very important to pay attention and listen to the instructions you are given by the judge about where to move your dog. Remember, even the most skilled handlers had to start somewhere. Keep it up and you too will become a proficient handler as you gain practice and experience.

accumulate 15 points at the shows from at least three different judges, including two "majors." A "major" is defined as a three-, four- or five-point win, and the number of points per win is determined on the number of dogs entered in the show on that day. Depending on the breed, the number of points that are awarded varies. In a breed as popular as the Boxer, more dogs are needed to rack up the points. At any dog show, only one dog and one bitch of each breed can win points.

Dog showing does not offer "co-ed" classes. Dogs and bitches

FIVE CLASSES AT SHOWS

At most AKC all-breed shows, there are five regular classes offered: Puppy, Novice, Bred-by-Exhibitor, American-bred and Open. The Puppy Class is usually divided as 6 to 9 months of age and 9 to 12 months of age. When deciding in which class to enter your dog, male or female, you must carefully check the show schedule to make sure that you have selected the right class. Depending on the age of the dog, previous first-place wins and the sex of the dog, you must make the best choice. It is possible to enter a one-year-old dog who has not won sufficient first places in any of the non-Puppy Classes, though the competition is more intense the further you progress from the Puppy Class.

never compete against each other in the classes. Non-champion dogs are called "class dogs" because they compete in one of five classes. Dogs are entered in a particular class depending on their age and previous show wins. To begin, there is the Puppy Class (for 6- to 9-month-olds and for 9- to 12-month-olds); this class is followed by the Novice Class (for dogs that have not won any first prizes except in the Puppy Class or three first prizes in the Novice Class and have not accumulated any points toward their champion title); the Bred-by-Exhibitor Class (for dogs handled by their breeders or handled by one of the breeder's immediate family); the American-bred Class (for dogs bred in the US!); and the Open Class (for any dog that is not a champion).

The judge at the show begins judging the Puppy Class, first dogs and then bitches, and proceeds through the classes. The judge places his winners first through fourth in each class. In the Winners Class, the first-place winners of each class compete with one another to determine Winners Dog and Winners Bitch. The judge also places a Reserve Winners Dog and Reserve Winners Bitch, which could be awarded the points in the case of a disqualification. The Winners Dog and Winners Bitch, the two that are

The famous Jacquet Boxer strain is known for its intelligence and sweet temperament as well as the wondrous expressions on the dogs' faces.

awarded the points for the breed, then compete with any champions of record entered in the show. The judge reviews the Winners Dog, Winners Bitch and all of the champions (often called "specials") to select his Best of Breed. The Best of Winners is

South African Ch. Osiris vom Okeler Forst illustrates a dog of slightly different appearance than European and American examples of the Boxer.

selected between the Winners Dog and Winners Bitch. Were one of these two to be selected Best of Breed, that dog would automatically be named Best of Winners as well. Finally the judge selects his Best of Opposite Sex to the Best of Breed winner.

At a Group show or all-breed show, the Best of Breed winners from each breed then compete against one another for Group One through Group Four. The judge compares each Best of Breed to his breed standard, and the dog that most closely lives up to the ideal for his breed is selected as Group One. Finally, all seven group winners (from the Working Group, Toy Group, Hound Group, etc.) compete for Best in Show.

To find out about dog shows in your area, you can subscribe to the American Kennel Club's monthly magazine, the *American Kennel Gazette* and the accompanying *Events Calendar*. You can also look in your local newspaper for advertisements for dog shows in your area or go on the Internet to the AKC's website, www.akc.org.

If your Boxer is six months of age or older and registered with the AKC, you can enter him in a dog show where the breed is offered classes. Provided that your Boxer does not have a disqualifying fault, he can compete. Only unaltered dogs can be entered in a dog show, so if you have spayed or neutered your Boxer, your dog cannot compete in conformation shows. The reason for this is simple. Dog shows are the main forum to prove which representatives in a breed are worthy of being bred. Only dogs that have achieved championships—the AKC "seal of approval" for quality in pure-bred dogs—-should be bred. Altered dogs, however, can participate in other AKC events such as obedience trials and the Canine Good Citizen® program.

ENTERING A DOG SHOW

Before you actually step into the ring, you would be well advised to sit back and observe the judge's ring procedure. If it is your first time in the ring, stand back and study how the exhibitor in front

Olimpio del Colle dell' Infinito, owned by Alessando Tanoni, is a wonderful example of the Italian-style Boxer.

of you is performing. The judge asks each handler to "stack" the dog, hopefully showing the dog off to his best advantage. The judge will observe the dog from a distance and from different angles, and approach the dog to check his teeth, overall structure, alertness and muscle tone, as well as consider how well the dog "conforms" to the standard. Most importantly, the judge will have the exhibitor move the dog around the ring in some pattern that he should specify (always listen since some judges change their directions—and the judge is always right!). Finally, the judge will give the dog one last look before moving on to the next exhibitor.

If you are not in the top four in your class at your first show, do not be discouraged. Be patient and consistent, and you may eventually find yourself in a winning line-up. Remember that

Sadeo Kikuchi's Japanese Ch. Cherry Heim Bushu Jacquet, bred out of American exports.

together. The pioneer of obedience trials is Mrs. Helen Whitehouse Walker, a Standard Poodle fancier, who designed a series of exercises after the Associated Sheep, Police Army Dog Society of Great Britain. Since the days of Mrs. Walker, obedience trials have grown by leaps and bounds, and today there are over 2,000 trials held in the US every year, with more than 100,000 dogs competing. Any AKC-registered dog can enter an obedience trial, regardless of conformational disqualifications or neutering.

Obedience trials are divided into three levels of progressive difficulty. At the first level, the Novice, dogs compete for the title Companion Dog (CD); at the intermediate level, the Open, dogs compete for the title Companion Dog Excellent (CDX);

Judges examine the Boxer's mouth to be sure that the bite is correct and that the teeth are present and in good condition.

the winners were once in your shoes and have devoted many hours and much money to earn the placement. If you find that your dog is losing every time and never getting a nod, it may be time to consider a different dog sport or to just enjoy your Boxer as a pet. Parent clubs offer other events, such as agility, tracking, obedience, instinct tests and more, which may be of interest to the owner of a well-trained Boxer.

OBEDIENCE TRIALS
Obedience trials in the US trace back to the early 1930s when organized obedience training was developed to demonstrate how well dog and owner could work

and at the advanced level, the Utility, dogs compete for the title Utility Dog (UD). Classes are subdivided into "A" (for beginners) and "B" (for more experienced handlers). A perfect score at any level is 200, and a dog must score 170 or better to earn a "leg," of which three are needed to earn the title. To earn points, the dog must score more than 50% of the available points in each exercise; the possible points range from 20 to 40.

Each level consists of a different set of exercises. In the Novice level, the dog must heel on- and off-lead, come, long sit, long down and stand for examination. These skills are the basic ones required for a well-behaved "Companion Dog." The Open level requires that the dog perform the same exercises as above but without a leash for extended lengths of time, as well as retrieve a dumbbell, broad jump and drop on recall. In the Utility level, dogs must perform ten difficult exercises, including scent discrimination, hand signals for basic commands, directed jump and directed retrieve.

Once a dog has earned the UD title, he can compete with other proven obedience dogs for the coveted title of Utility Dog Excellent (UDX), which requires that the dog win "legs" in ten shows. Utility Dogs who earn "legs" in Open B and Utility B earn points

Ch. Newlaithe Marietta, owned by Christine Beardsell of Huddersfield, England.

Newlaithe Tex Style, shown here at seven months of age, is owned by Christine and Pat Beardsell. This is a typical high-quality British youngster.

toward their Obedience Trial Champion title. In 1977 the title Obedience Trial Champion (OTCh.) was established by the AKC. To become an OTCh., a dog needs to earn 100 points, which requires three first places in Open B and Utility under three different judges.

The Grand Prix of obedience trials, the AKC National Obedience Invitational gives qualifying Utility Dogs the chance to win the newest and highest title: National Obedience Champion (NOC). Only the top 25 ranked obedience dogs, plus any dog ranked in the top 3 in his breed, are allowed to compete.

A lovely Boxer from the West coast, shown by Patti Rutledge.

TRACKING

Any dog is capable of tracking, using his nose to follow a trail. Tracking tests are exciting and competitive ways to test your Boxer's ability to search and rescue. The AKC started tracking tests in 1937, when the first AKC-licensed test took place as part of the Utility level at an obedience trial. Ten years later in 1947, the AKC offered the first title, Tracking Dog (TD). It was not until 1980 that the AKC added the Tracking Dog Excellent title (TDX), which was followed by the Versatile Surface Tracking title (VST) in 1995. The title Champion Tracker (CT) is awarded to a dog who has earned all three titles.

In the beginning level of tracking, the owner follows the dog through a field on a long lead. To earn the TD title, the dog must follow a track laid by a human 30 to 120 minutes prior. The track is about 500 yards with up to 5 directional changes. The TDX requires that the dog follow a track that is 3 to 5 hours old over a course up to 1,000 yards with up to 7 directional changes. The VST requires that the dog follow a track up to 5 hours old through an urban setting.

AGILITY TRIALS

Having had its origins in the UK back in 1977, AKC agility had its official beginning in the US in August 1994, when the first licensed agility trials were held. The AKC allows all registered breeds (including Miscellaneous Class breeds) to participate, providing the dog is 12 months of age or older. Agility is designed so that the handler demonstrates how well the dog can work at his side. The handler directs his dog over an obstacle course that includes jumps as well as tires, the dog walk, weave poles, pipe tunnels, collapsed tunnels, etc. While working his way through the course, the dog must keep one eye and ear on the handler and the rest of his body on the course. The handler gives verbal commands and hand signals to guide the dog through the course.

The first organization to promote agility trials in the US

was the United States Dog Agility Association, Inc. (USDAA), which was established in 1986 and spawned numerous member clubs around the country. Both the USDAA and the AKC offer titles to winning dogs. Three titles are available through the USDAA: Agility Dog (AD), Advanced Agility Dog (AAD) and Master Agility Dog (MAD). The AKC offers Novice Agility (NA), Open Agility (OA), Agility Excellent (AX) and Master Agility Excellent (MX). Beyond these four AKC titles, dogs can win additional ones in "jumper" classes, Jumpers with Weave Novice (NAJ), Open (OAJ) and Excellent (MXJ), which lead to the ultimate title(s): MACH, Master Agility Champion. Dogs can continue to add number designations to the MACH titles, indicating how many times the

dog has met the MACH requirements, such as MACH1, MACH2.

Agility is great fun for dog and owner, with many rewards for everyone involved. Interested owners should join a training club that has obstacles and experienced agility handlers who can introduce you and your dog to the "ropes" (and tires, tunnels, etc.).

The Canine Good Citizen® program is a wonderful experience for both you and your dog.

Practice makes *titled* perfection! Obedience, agility, tracking...is there anything the Boxer can't achieve?

INDEX

My Boxer

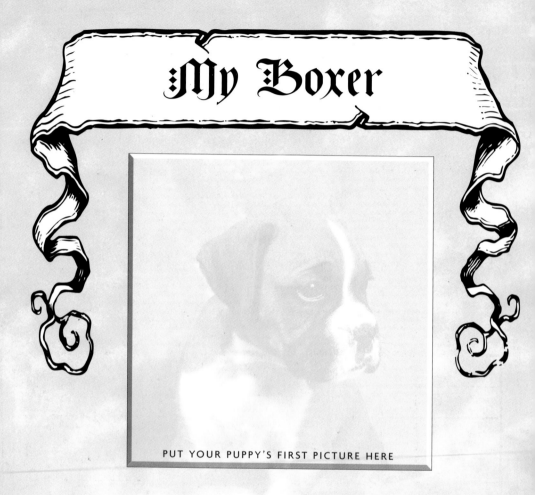

PUT YOUR PUPPY'S FIRST PICTURE HERE

Dog's Name _____

Date _____ Photographer _____